WHAT LEADERS ARE SAYING ABOUT
DOGS DON'T BARK AT PARKED CARS

I will include *Dogs Don't Bark at Parked Cars* on a list of life lesson books for my young sons to read. Jeff and Eric created a motivational guide for business success through the blizzard of distractions called the Information Age. Entertaining stories, analogies, and insights from business giants illustrate the core values and actions needed to create business success, which is the foundation of any thriving community. We are reminded there is no victory that isn't shared, and the most important person to motivate and manage is in the mirror.

Jeffrey Holder, Certified Business Performance Advisor
Insperity, Inc.

This book delivers useful insights from highly successful business leaders who had the courage to face the barking dogs. This is a must-read for those who desire to succeed and lead. I have read many books on success and business management and have found none that captured my interest like this one. Just read it and see!

Joseph Duda, CEO and Chairman
A. Duda & Sons (Retired)

Sometimes we need a dog nipping at our heels to get us moving. So, analyze your opportunities, choose carefully, and then move positively forward, never giving up. The harder you work, the luckier you will be! Reading this book will make your hard work luckier.

B.W. "Bernie" Simpkins, Entrepreneur and CEO
S&S Enterprises

T0124550

As a life-long friend of the writer, I read this book with special knowledge. I also read it as a bank executive who has had relationships with entrepreneurs for well over 30 years. I have seen the very successful to the not-so-successful. The authors take their successful experiences highlighting core competencies and personal insight to pass on to another generation. It won't guarantee your success but will send you on the right path.

Robert Powell, Senior Vice President and Commercial Business Manager

I have known Jeff for over 40 years. The lessons reflected in *Dogs Don't Bark at Parked Cars* speak to his hallmark high energy and passion for life. This is a great primer for any leader.

H.H. "Butch" Howard III, Captain
United States Navy (Retired)

Dogs Don't Bark at Parked Cars is a motivational guidebook written for entrepreneurs and individuals wanting to set up or improve their business practices. Anecdotes, featuring "man's best friend," introduce and illustrate the subject of each chapter. These scenarios connect with the reader and help make the principle of the chapter memorable. This book is more than a training manual — it is a guide on interpersonal relationships and living a positive, inspirational life - no matter what your career.

Dr. Katherine Piersall, Ed.D, Educator and Principal
Florida Educational Curriculum Director - Elementary (Retired)

In the easily read pages of *Dogs Don't Bark at Parked Cars*, Jeff Piersall and Eric Wright have woven a tapestry of quotes and real-life examples from the experiences of past, current, and future local, state, national and international leaders. The attributes these leaders acquired and demonstrated are carefully and thoroughly defined and illustrated. To embrace Jeff and Eric's metaphor, if you spend a few hours experiencing their narrative, you will be "barking up the right tree!"

Randy Berridge, CEO
Florida's High Tech Corridor

This book is about more than entrepreneurship and business—it is about life and life's lessons. So, read, reflect and apply. But mostly, simply enjoy.

J. Stanley "Stan" Payne, C–Level Executive, Attorney and Corporate Strategist

Jeff and Eric created a masterpiece. In business and life, there are principles and practices. Principles are timeless, and practices are timely. This is a compilation of many principles everyone should execute. This is a must-read. Dawn and I highly recommend this book become a part of your library!

Joe and Dawn Pici, Owners
Pici and Pici, Inc.

I spent my career endeavoring to impart character and life skills to young people to carry with them throughout life. *Dogs Don't Bark at Parked Cars* is a thoughtful and entertaining presentation of key character qualities and life skills, which shape the journey of the entrepreneur and transcend generations and professions. It is a must-read!

Ron Oates, Southern Regional Director and Chief Diversity Officer
Boy Scouts of America

Steve Jobs taught us "some things need to be believed to be seen." Entrepreneurs believe before they see and are of themselves seeds of big ideas. Jeff and Eric help you see with great clarity by providing a thoughtful, entertaining, and personally useful way to view how to navigate a start-up to bring a big idea to market … or help an established enterprise make its way in the world. There is an old saying, "if you want milk you'd best not sit on a stool in the middle of a field and hope a cow backs up to you." Jeff and Eric help you act on your ideas, big and small. Whether the dogs are barking at you or you are looking for a road map as you build your ideas, they will help guide you through the world of successful entrepreneurship … even in Kansas … with no stool needed.

Rick Walsh, CEO, The Knob Hill Companies
Chairman Emeritus, UCF Board of Trustees
SVP Corporate Affairs, Darden Restaurants (Retired)

Jeff and Eric provide ten proven virtues to build a successful business through a perspective that can only be provided because they have truly been on all sides of the table: entrepreneurs, business mentors and publishers of highly successful business magazines, routinely interacting with top business leaders. *Dogs Don't Bark at Parked Cars* is a highly enjoyable book delivered with a great balance of down-home common sense and actionable advice.

Mark Mohler, President
Corridor Legal

Dogs Don't Bark at Parked Cars unleashes strong leadership in our dog-eat-dog world!

Laura Joslin, CEO, Ability Plus Therapy
Founder, No Limits Academy

In *Dogs Don't Bark at Parked Cars*, Jeff and Eric speak to the entrepreneur in all of us. They offer lessons transcending both cultures and generations. I have seen this wisdom at work throughout my career from my first technology startups to my involvement with TEDx. In this day of constant change, it's important to remember that some things are timeless.

Alex Rudloff, Partner
More Than Theory

Building and scaling your own business is the hardest job you'll ever love. To succeed, you must be a lifelong learner adapting to a rapidly changing market. You must also develop the people skills enabling you to lead and interface with every conceivable people type. *Dogs Don't Bark At Parked Cars* is one of the best books I've found on how to do both, and there aren't two better examples of this than Eric and Jeff.

Sam Pak, CEO
Appliance Direct

This book should be a required read for anyone considering becoming an entrepreneur or looking to take charge of their life. By putting the many "bones" of wisdom shared in this book into practice, you are immediately better positioned to achieve your goals by leveraging the hard-earned lessons of successful people who have already done it.

Travis Proctor, CEO
Artemis

During my forty-five years as a bank president and CEO, I have observed many business clients that would have benefited from the wisdom found in *Dogs Don't Bark at Parked Cars*. Personally, as an avid reader of Dr. Norman Vincent Peale, Zig Ziglar, Dr. Robert Schuller, and Napoleon Hill; I found myself wishing this masterpiece produced by Jeff and Eric had been available decades ago. It would have helped my clients, my employees, and me tremendously. I highly recommend the wisdom in these pages to aspiring leaders and their teams.

J. Lamar Roberts, President and CEO, Fidelity Bank of Florida
Past President, Florida Bankers Association

Jeff and Eric have always inspired and motivated me with their dedication to helping others get ahead in life. Both Jeff and Eric are an inspiration on how to deal with the ups and downs of life and what it takes to keep moving forward to reach your life goals and be successful, personally and professionally.

Scott Sorensen, CEO
Sorensen Moving & Storage

If you read any book this year about entrepreneurship, read *Dogs Don't Bark at Parked Cars*. While most books explain the "how," Eric and Jeff delve into the heart of the entrepreneur. It contains real-world stories that confront the issues anyone who wants to live the American dream will face.

Waymon Armstrong, Founder and CEO
Engineering & Computer Simulations

While I enjoyed the earthy realism of Jeff and Eric's approach to entrepreneurialism, don't let those dog metaphors fool you. Juxtaposed to those colloquialisms are keen, razor-sharp insights on success, what it takes, and how to get there.

Lynda Weatherman, CEO
Economic Development Commission of Florida's Space Coast

Dogs Don't Bark at Parked Cars speaks to the heart of entrepreneurship and, more importantly, to the hearts of the entrepreneurs themselves. The authors excel at storytelling with a focus on the less tangible parts of entrepreneurship — values, legacy, fear, diversity, and more. Cleverly comparing current and would-be entrepreneurs with our canine companions, chapter titles like "Running Without a Leash" and "Be the Person Your Dog Thinks You Are" make this book a clever, fun, and thoughtful read.

Penny Lewandowski, Vice President of External Relations and Strategic Direction, Edward Lowe Foundation

Dogs Don't Bark at Parked Cars

DOGS DON'T
BARK
AT PARKED CARS

Your GPS in an Era of Hyper-Change

JEFF PIERSALL & ERIC WRIGHT

NEW YORK

NASHVILLE • MELBOURNE • VANCOUVER

Dogs Don't Bark at Parked Cars
Your GPS in an Era of Hyper-Change

© 2018 Trep. LLC

Published in New York, New York, by Morgan James Publishing. Morgan James is a trademark of Morgan James, LLC. www.MorganJamesPublishing.com

The Morgan James Speakers Group can bring authors to your live event. For more information or to book an event visit The Morgan James Speakers Group at www.TheMorganJamesSpeakersGroup.com.

ISBN 9781683504467 paperback
ISBN 9781683504474 eBook
Library of Congress Control Number: 2017901733

Cover Design by:
SCB Marketing

Interior Design by:
Chris Treccani
www.3dogcreative.net

In an effort to support local communities, raise awareness and funds, Morgan James Publishing donates a percentage of all book sales for the life of each book to Habitat for Humanity Peninsula and Greater Williamsburg.

Get involved today! Visit
www.MorganJamesBuilds.com

ACKNOWLEDGMENTS

The familiar phrase, "Behind every good man is a great woman," doesn't apply to the authors. In our case, our wives, Susan and Judy, are not behind us; in most cases, they are way out in front, and our relationship to them is our greatest accomplishment. We would not be where we are, nor will we get where we want to go, without their love, support and belief in us. They provide a compass of firm reliance on the Lord for us to follow.

John C. Maxwell once said, "Teamwork makes the dream work." We want to express our gratitude to our team and the many individuals who offered support, encouragement, and inspiration throughout this journey. We would like to thank Morgan James Publishing for believing in us and acquiring this book. To our publicist and agent, Wendy Kurtz, for guiding us throughout the process. To our SCB Marketing team and project manager, Alisha Crabtree, for helping create a movement. To Joseph Duda for your example, leadership and belief in us. And lastly, to all the individuals who helped inspire this book with your authentic stories of courage and success.

DEDICATION

Dogs Don't Bark at Parked Cars is dedicated to the TREP spirits who dream big despite failures, setbacks and barking dogs. The ones who believe in the impossible; yet, make it happen.

en**TREP**reneur

*"Any individual who created or is leading a sustainable,
scalable, and growth-oriented organization or company."*

CONTENTS

FOREWORD

When they write the history, and do the theses on the growth and development of entrepreneurialism in Florida; one leader is sure to be included: Dr. Tom O'Neal. The University of Central Florida's vice president of research and commercialization, Tom is recognized throughout the nation as a pioneering innovator and the founder and executive director of the UCF Business Incubator Program. He was also instrumental in the National Business Incubation Association, moving its headquarters and global training center to the UCF Research Park. If that wasn't enough, he also founded the Florida Economic Gardening Institute, known as GrowFL. Since 1999, it has helped hundreds of companies create thousands of new jobs, which have had an annual economic impact of more than $510 million, with an average salary of $59,000. Their "Florida Companies to Watch" is the most celebrated recognition of second-stage companies in the state. In addition, Tom has been a great inspiration and ally in our entrepreneurial journey.

— The Authors

I initially came to Orlando and the University of Central Florida to work at CREOL, the Center for Research and Education in Optics and Lasers. As an electrical engineer with an MBA, I soon became involved in starting a company along with a CREOL faculty member, and then a second business with another member of the faculty. Launching those businesses gave me firsthand insight into what we call the "Valley of Death," the gap between cutting-edge university research and its practical application in the market. It was an experience that moved me into the business incubation arena back in 1999.

My fundamental notion was the greatest technology in the world doesn't do anyone any good if it stays in a lab—or even if it moves to a patent stage but is then put on a shelf in what I call a "pawn shop model," hoping someone will come along and bring it to market. I ended up doing my doctoral dissertation looking at economic ecosystems. I discovered the crucial role incubators play in filling a gap in the business development process. During this time, people began to realize jobs are created by entrepreneurs who produce scalable businesses. If you increase the success rate of these ventures, everyone wins.

At the same time, the college and university system has undergone a significant and remarkable change in the last ten years. Rather than being an ivory tower institution, UCF has done incredible work in and with the community. The university is active in developing companies and even created one of the first venture capital funds. States are making huge capital investments in education, and now would like to see a direct return on that investment in the form of jobs.

I studied incubators across the country and around the world. I was introduced to individuals who were incredibly open and giving. They weren't competing; instead, they wanted to partner for everyone's mutual success. They embodied the principles Jeff and Eric articulate in *Dogs Don't Bark at Parked Cars*.

All incubators, starter spaces, and early-stage venture funds have one primary purpose: to foster great businesses. If you produce successful businesses, everything else takes care of itself. They create jobs and bring in capital. When that happens, infrastructure improves; cultural venues are funded; and, educational institutions flourish. Frankly, everyone's quality of life goes up. It is the tide that lifts all the boats in the harbor. It all works when you focus on one thing: creating businesses.

The best way I have found to achieve that end is to encourage entrepreneurial development and even an entrepreneurial mindset in those engaged in the corporate world. It fosters freedom, fulfillment, and creativity, both for the entrepreneur and for those who work with and for them. What's more, these entrepreneurs, in turn, reinvest back into their community philanthropically and are actively engaged in funding and mentoring other new businesses.

America's greatness lies in our ability to adapt to new conditions with innovation and enthusiasm. That spirit of innovation and enthusiasm, combined with a perseverance and entrepreneurial culture, is what made America so prosperous for so long. It continues to play out daily in small, young startup companies across the country.

The philosophy of free enterprise and entrepreneurialism is founded on personal responsibility, values-based ethical decisions, and a sky's-the-limit optimism, which is exactly what *Dogs Don't Bark at Parked Cars* explains and promotes. This is our best hope for a bright economic future, not only in our state but across the country and around the world.

—**Tom O'Neal, Ph.D.**

Associate Vice President of Research and Commercialization at the University of Central Florida (UCF)
Executive Director of the UCF Business Incubation Program (UCFBIP)
Executive Director of the Florida Economic Gardening Institute (FEGI)

INTRODUCTION

It's easy to avoid criticism: All you have to do is say nothing,
do nothing, be nothing.
—Aristotle

"It was summer of 1969 in Winchester, Kentucky," Jeff Piersall recalls, "and at the impulsive and overconfident age of ten, my friends and I roamed the town, playing cops and robbers, or some other heroic game. In those days, the entire city limits were our boundaries, and our version of *The Fast and the Furious* was played out on Husky Stingray bicycles.

On any typical day, eight to twelve of us would depart from my house on Fitch Avenue in the morning and, except for stopping back to inhale lunch, not return until the street lights came on signaling it was time for dinner. We rode those bikes all day, chasing and trying to catch each other through the streets. For us, the only bad guys in our world were what we pretended the kids on the other team were that day.

But there was one street that was a no-fly zone, even though it was a shortcut to almost everywhere. The reason was simple. On that road was the biggest Dalmatian you have ever seen, a regular Steven King *Cujo*. In my mind, his head had to be three-and-a-half feet from the ground. He would ferociously chase any bike or car; in fact, anything moving through his designated territory was a target, and his bark was menacing.

On this particular day, I decided I was faster and tougher than that old dog, and I wasn't going to keep taking the long way around. Similarly, in life we all have goals we want to reach, visions we feel destined to fulfill, and invariably there is something blocking our way. In this case, it was a Dalmatian on steroids. So, mustering all my bravado, I was going to run the gauntlet knowing he would come after me. But hey, none of my friends could catch me, so I figured I could beat this dog.

It must have been adrenaline that sent me into hyper drive as I pedaled like I never had before. However, as he got closer, instead of keeping my head down and making a beeline to the other end of the street, where he seemed to have an invisible boundary that would always stop him, my attention drifted from the end of the street to the hound at the rear end of my bike. Abandoning my plan and my greatest asset, *speed,* and thinking I could take on the Kentucky version of *The Hound of the Baskervilles,* I kicked at him.

The only thing I made contact with was the air. Within a nanosecond, his teeth were firmly fastened onto my ten-year-old left buttock. I had been bitten by the barking dog. OUCH!"

Timeless Lessons It Took Time to Learn

Dogs don't bark at parked cars. They only chase moving objects. If you pay attention to them and slow down ... you got it ... they can bite. For dogs, stationary objects like fire hydrants and mailboxes have a completely different purpose in their universe.

As an entrepreneurial leader, being stationary is not what you are made for—and you aren't running away from something, but toward something. However, if you are moving, you are going to attract attention. Regrettably, it isn't always positive.

The people who bark at our desire to initiate, create, and innovate can often be debilitating. To make matters worse, the bark of these seemingly well-meaning and supposedly well-informed individuals can cast a pall over the best idea or cause the most courageous soul to falter, only because they seem to be in a position of knowledge.

Consider what Jim Denny, the manager of the Grand Ole Opry, said when he fired Elvis Presley: "You ain't going nowhere, son. You ought to go back to driving a truck."

After decades of entrepreneurial experience and interviewing hundreds of successful innovators and CEOs, we have discovered ten qualities the most effective trailblazers and dog out-runners share. We aren't talking about aptitude or talent. Those are easy to identify and monetize. They are part of what defines us and our entrepreneurial trajectory. Instead, these are changeless qualities in an era of uber-change.

1. The Foundation of Trust
2. Relational Priority
3. Diversity of Expression
4. Influence, Not Imposition
5. The Significance of Synergy
6. Prevailing Vision
7. Process Orientation
8. Validating Desire
9. Recognizing Life is Both Natural and Spiritual
10. Building a Legacy

Can You See the Pattern?

Intelligence is often identified by the ability to recognize patterns and outcomes in numbers: 2, 4, 6 ... 8; in categories: George Washington, John Adams, Thomas Jefferson ... James Madison. The same is true in a successful leader's behavior. We have seen these principles over and over, and they all end up equaling the same thing: a successful career and life. What's more, in countless ways, these are the things that will save you time and money. Each one is like a slat in a barrel; take out one or take out part of one and the barrel's capacity drops to that level.

They provide an inner compass giving direction regardless of your situation and a perspective that isn't mired by emotions or trends of the immediate. It is like the Egyptian proverb, "The **barking** of a **dog** does not disturb the man on a camel." After reading this book you won't be on a camel, but you will have a higher perspective that will keep your eye on where you want to go, instead of on the dogs nipping at your heels.

One of the reasons these changeless qualities are so important is that we live in an era where change is taking place more rapidly than at any time in human history. It has been observed from the time of Jesus and Caesar to the time of the American Revolution, the way most people lived changed very little. They rode horses or traveled in ships propelled by the wind, they cooked over fires and communicated with letters. Sure, we developed the printing press, harnessed gunpowder, invented the telescope, and advanced our understanding of the universe, but the way we did life was largely unaltered.

From the American Revolution to the American Civil War, in less than 100 years, technology advanced as much as it had in the previous 2,000 years. Locomotives and steamships changed transportation, and telegraphs carried messages across continents. Between the 1870s and World War I, it happened again. The Theory of Relativity was developed, telephones were becoming commonplace, heavier-than-air flight was a new normal, and automobiles were replacing horses. It happened again by the beginning of the next World War and it continued to accelerate. Technologists today believe as remarkable as computers, cellphones, and the Internet are, we have about 10 percent of the technology that will change the not-too-distant future.

In this era of amazing change, we have to be creative, nimble, and adaptive. But thoughtful leaders have to root their lives and their businesses in things that don't change, in values that can stand the test of time and won't be as obsolete as the phone you thought was a wonder and is now in a box in your closet. As Stephen Hawking said, "Our future is a race between the growing power of technology and the wisdom with which we use it."

Entrepreneurial Generation

Millennials with their entrepreneurial spirit are the opportunity for everyone's future. They have the chance to bring balance to the work, life, and spirit equation. They are digital natives, whereas even the most tech-savvy Baby Boomers are analog natives and digital immigrants (who fixes the remote after the power goes out?). However, they are not always wiser because wisdom comes from experience.

Someone once challenged the old adage "Experience is the best teacher," contending instead "The experience of others is the best teacher." There are two important sources of wisdom: your experience and the experience of others. You don't have to learn everything through trial and error. Advances—whether they are social, technological, or organizational—progress rapidly from the lessons and discoveries of others and not, as they say, "by reinventing the wheel." Instead, use the wheel idea someone else came up with and take it from there.

The purpose of this book is to share the wisdom of those who have not only run the race but have won. Our passion is that you learn from their lessons (like Jeff, "keep your eye on the goal, not the barking dog, and definitely don't try to kick at one") and apply their discoveries to your life.

The price of personal experience, though often more real and memorable, comes at a high cost, and at times the collateral damage can be great. To avoid those ever-inflating costs, learn from some of the best who have paid the price themselves and are usually delighted to share their most valuable resource: the wisdom they have gained through experience.

If you are in the entrepreneurial hunt or are considering it as the best means of achieving independence in your life; this book is for you. We are convinced next to dogs; entrepreneurialism may be man's best friend.

Without the resistance of the wind, the eagle does not soar. Without the resistance of the water, the boat does not float. Without the resistance of gravity, you and I can't walk. Without opposition or resistance, there is no potential for growth.

Throughout the course of this book, we will pause for

which are insights encouraging reflection.

1. **Sources of Wisdom:** There are two important sources of wisdom: your experience and the experience of others. Have you learned trial and error isn't the shortest path to your goals, but instead it is learning from the trials, errors, and successes of others? Can you recall seeing another's mistake that helped you avoid one yourself?

2. **Reputation vs. Character:** Reputation is how others perceive you, which begs the question, "Can you control how others think about you?" The answer is no. Therefore, investing in your reputation is a poor investment; it is impression management. Instead, invest in your character

daily. Ultimately, your character is the fundamental that determines your reputation.

3. **Have the mindset of a TREP:** (an abbreviated term for "en**trep**reneur")

    D. You are "constitutionally unemployable," though you should be the best employee a business has. You can't resist the opportunity of setting your own course.

    E. You do not want to depend on others for your financial well-being.

    F. You understand giving value to others first will bring you all you need.

    G. Remember, the mind and a parachute are the same. They must be open to work. So, open up and take in the sights and sounds of this book. It will make your journey more fruitful.

4. **Who is this book for?** "The credit belongs to those who are actually in the arena, who strive valiantly; who know the great enthusiasm, the great devotions, and spend themselves in a worthy cause; who at the best, know the triumph of high achievement; and who, at the worst, if they fail, fail while daring greatly, so that their place shall never be with those cold and timid souls who never know neither victory nor defeat."

    —Theodore Roosevelt

CHAPTER 1

What the Dog Whispered
The Foundation of Trust

No low-trust society will ever produce sustained innovation.
—Thomas L. Friedman, *The World is Flat*

Have you ever sat in an airport and watched someone who is visually impaired being led by a dog? Perhaps you've heard accounts from soldiers whose lives were saved because a dog detected an IED and risked its life to save others.

Orlando was Cecil Williams' guide dog. One day, 61-year-old Williams passed out while waiting for the subway in New York and his black labrador sprang into action. Orlando grabbed hold of Williams and tried to keep him from falling, but was unable to stop him from tumbling onto the tracks. So, the dog tried to alert other passengers to the danger by barking. When that didn't work, he jumped onto the tracks and started licking Williams in an attempt to wake him. "He went down, and the dog jumped down," an eyewitness told the *New York Post.* "He wasn't pulled. He was kissing him trying to get him to move."

Williams came to just as an express train was entering the station. The subway workers, who arrived on the scene, told him to hide in the "trough" in the middle of the tracks. Then the train ran over Williams and his dog. Miraculously, they survived with only minor injuries.

The "whys" behind the remarkable relationship between humans and our canine companions is something scientists and dog lovers are just beginning to understand. Those who seem to grasp canine behavior and relate to dogs best we call "whisperers." But what would our dogs like to whisper to us?

One thing is clear: The same behaviors and needs solidifying the bonds between people and dogs make business endeavors work as well. Business isn't just about technology, know-how, or innovative products and services. It is about people and the relationships built between them. There is but one glue holding that relationship together, whether it is the person who does our dry cleaning or the one we're shaking hands with to consummate a multimillion-dollar transaction. That quality is trust.

Consider the English bulldog. Today, this breed is known mostly as a college mascot. In pre-industrial England, the breed was developed for farming. What do you suppose they were used for? To protect the farmer from the bull when he was trying to feed or work around these often belligerent and unpredictable animals. If the bull turned to gore the farmer, it was the bulldog who subdued the bull by biting him on the nose or ear. The bulldog held on until the bull submitted. Because of the nature of their job, bulldogs were bred to have powerful, muscular bodies. Their resolve to hold onto a huge raging bull, even when injured, is extraordinary.

That kind of trust demonstration is unforgettable in an animal or a colleague. In a very real sense, the farmer put his life in the dog's hands, and to a lesser degree, we put our enterprises and futures in the hands of those with whom we do business. When you think about it, this entire global system of commerce is not based on monetary policies or trade agreements; these are just symbols or manifestations of this core quality of trust.

Every entrepreneur, "starter" or "trep," engages in a journey leading to unprecedented heights and at times to lows most didn't dream possible. Like Dickens' famous opening to *A Tale of Two Cities*, "It was the best of times, it was the worst of times." There is discovery, adventure, risk and reward. There are also challenges you face that stretch the fabric of your being and the tensile strength of your trust and, equally important, your ability to remain trustworthy.

The most important lessons in that process are the insights and wisdom to be gained on both sides of this "*best of*" and "*worst of*" coin. The challenges or setbacks aren't enemies; they are portals of insight and opportunity making all aspects of the journey significant. Also, these experiences aren't electives we choose, nor are they classes we can skip. But they are subjects we can pass quickly. For Eric Wright, the following was one of those classes. It was graduate school in the art of trust, and it is etched on his mind and character forever.

From Africa to ICU

Though we would later become friends, it was the first time I met Dr. Robert (Bob) Purser, a radiologist with surgical intervention as a specialty. As he introduced himself, I thought he looked pensive, like he had drawn the short straw.

The year was 1994, and when Dr. Purser came into my wife Susan's room in the intensive care ward, which had become our home for the last few weeks, I could sense his discomfort and understood why. Just a few days before, her cardiologist had pulled me aside in the hospital hall and said, "I know you are a man of faith, but someone has to be honest with you. You need to prepare yourself for the worst." I felt I had been caught in the swirling vortex of a whirlpool with absolutely no power to break free or to change the outcome of a situation that daily seemed to go from bad to worse.

Two-and-a-half weeks earlier, we returned from a dream vacation in Africa. My son John William, eleven at the time, actually had tears in his eyes as the van carrying my family drove the dusty roads for the last time to the aircraft that would fly us from Livingston in Zambia to Johannesburg and home. For three magical weeks, we had toured the most magnificent game parks in South Africa, Zimbabwe, and Zambia. But unknown to any of us, Susan was bringing something home none of us knew about, which would test our lives, our character, and our trust.

Days after we arrived home, Susan developed what we assumed was a case of the flu, which is not uncommon in international travel. Her fever seemed to come and go, but when my seven-year-old son, Quentin, called me at my office and said, "Something's wrong with mommy, she doesn't make sense," I rushed home and found her lying in bed where I had left her that morning. She was slumped to the side and made unintelligible responses to my questions.

I immediately carried her to the emergency room in my car. The on-call physician, having asked a few diagnostic questions like "Have you traveled abroad recently?" immediately diagnosed her as having malaria. My father had contracted malaria in the Pacific in World War II, like many soldiers there, so I wasn't too worried.

However, what any South African physician would know, but this doctor and none who attended her for the next two days knew, was she had a rare form of malaria called falciparum or "black water fever." It comes from the fact that the victim's urine turns almost black as the body tries to dispose of dead red blood cells. If it isn't aggressively treated, it has an almost 100 percent mortality rate.

Seeing how quickly her situation was deteriorating, she was transferred to the ICU at a larger hospital. The case was taken over by a close friend at that time, Dr. David Weldon, who would later go on to be a four-term U.S. Congressman. Soon, Susan digressed into what they called "multisystem organ failure." Her kidneys, lungs, and digestive tract shut down.

A day later, they did a tracheotomy and a catheter was put in her heart to help ease treatment. Another tube was put in her arm for kidney dialysis and the countless injections and IVs she got throughout the day and night.

We were living from hour to hour. I had never been in a hospital overnight, even when our sons were born. Now I felt I knew the medical staff and the almost 20 physicians who attended her like old friends. In the days before Facebook or the Internet, somehow people from around the world got news of Susan's condition and flooded me with cards and prayers.

Dr. Weldon would later tell me, "She was the sickest patient I ever had who lived." He came to me that day and said, "We have arrested the malaria. Now, we just have to keep her alive long enough for her body to recover. But there seems to be an infection somewhere, and we can't pinpoint it." God only knows how, but her heart was holding strong, and we hoped her brain wasn't damaged by the organ-clogging effects of the disease. Now, this new infection was the concern. This was why Dr. Purser was there to talk with me.

He explained to me that she was too sick to move to the surgical unit or for doctors to try and remove her gallbladder. The only alternative was to bring a portable X-ray machine into her room and use it to insert a catheter. He knew it was extremely risky at best and didn't want to be the last physician to treat her before she died.

I asked what her chances were if we did nothing. In a very diplomatic way, he said they were slim to none.

Dr. Weldon was one of the smartest guys I knew with impeccable character. He insisted on this direction with resounding confidence and trust in Dr. Purser, even to the point of assuming responsibility. But the decision was mine. "So, we have no choice here, doctor?" I half stated and half inquired as Dr. Purser explained the procedure. It was time to let go and simply trust.

I trusted Dave, and because of his trust in Dr. Purser, I felt I could trust him as well. I didn't ask for his credentials, a history of his surgical experience, or a percentage breakdown of other patients who had been in this situation that he had treated. Trust saved my wife hours, if not days, of costly delays.

Fortunately, the procedure was a success, though Susan was in a coma for six weeks. It was a full year before she made a complete recovery. Today, more than twenty years later, she shows no evidence of the horrific ordeal. It was an experience that taught the two of us many life lessons, but one of the most significant was about the power of trust.

Most of our business decisions aren't a matter of life or death, but it may mean the life of your company, your dream, or your relationship with a business partner or client. Thus, trust becomes the key to every relationship we build.

The Power of Trust

People often think "trust" is some soft, intangible skill, but the fact of the matter is more than anything else, trust saves you time and resources. It is the one value that, when present, ensures decision-making is easy and reduces the sense of risk in any transaction.

As Stephen M.R. Covey said in his classic book *The Speed of Trust*: "Trust is an economic driver, not just a social virtue. It's an ability to collaborate, to innovate, to attract and retain people, to satisfy, to engage, to execute your strategy. High trust pays dividends; low trust is a tax … Trust is the common denominator in every relationship, every business, every family, and every culture. It is the one thing that changes everything."

Consider how trust affects every transaction. Refinancing a home mortgage used to take weeks, if you had good credit and a healthy loan-to-value percentage. Now, it can be worse than an IRS audit and take months. Why the hassle, not to mention the time and expense the bank goes through to close a simple loan, which it may already have on its books? Because of the legislation passed after the banking crisis of 2008. When trust is low, everything slows down and costs more money.

How many of you remember flying before September 11, 2001? Since then, you need to arrive a minimum of two hours early on domestic flights and three hours for international travel. The Transportation Security Administration (TSA) has a budget of $7.4 billion. The Burj Khalifa, the world's tallest building in Dubai, has an estimated cost of $1.5 billion. That means we could build five of those a year across the fruited plains on the TSA budget! Instead, that money and time is added, like a tax, to every flight in the U.S.

A lack of trust causes business deals, even relationships, to feel like you are walking across a frozen lake on very thin ice.

Trust is based on two essential ingredients: integrity (character) and ability (competence). When we know someone's character is based on unchanging principles, we have the same confidence in that person's dependability as we do in a bridge we cross daily in our commute or the switch we use to turn on a light. When people are competent, we trust their ability, just as we trust that of pilots when we put our lives in their hands every time we board a plane.

When character or competence is questioned, everything slows down, and confidence gives way to hesitant and calculated caution. Small compromises can cause clients, partners, and subordinates to ask the question, "Will he (or she) do that to me?" The inability of a mechanic to fix your car or a package service to deliver your parcel replaces certainty with questions, if not fears. Character forms the groundwork of our lives, and if it is flawed, eventually it will get exposed.

Like Warren Buffett's comment about recessions, "You find out who is swimming naked when the tide goes out."

Everything positive is built on the foundation of trust. When we think of a foundation, we are describing something that isn't always seen, but its lack is clearly evident. The most famous tower in the world, besides the Eiffel Tower in Paris, isn't known for its height, style, or age; but because before it was even completed, it started to shift on its foundation. When a foundation is bad, like it was with the Leaning Tower of Pisa, you must engage in Herculean efforts to compensate for its flaws or tear it down and start all over.

When trust is broken, a chasm is created that is more difficult to fill than the Grand Canyon. Mahatma Gandhi once said, "The moment there is suspicion about a person's motives, everything he does becomes tainted." On the other hand, the trust that comes from knowing someone's character and competence removes hesitancy and makes a handshake as good as a ream of documents prepared by lawyers.

Sometimes, we overlook the significance of these qualities on the trust equation and opt for either, "Well, she's a good person" or "I know he is a little shady, but he's the best of the best." Eric's reliance on Dr. Purser wasn't because he was a good or honest man. Eric had never met him and couldn't have known that. It was because he was competent to perform the procedure that saved his wife's life. So, he trusted him.

However, it is obvious the leaders of Enron were competent. The book and movie chronicling their rise and fall was called *The Smartest Guys in the Room*. They just didn't have the combination of character and competence providing the foundation of trust.

It is also vital to note our trust is transferable, like a bearer bond we give to someone else as collateral. Eric's trust was in Dr. Weldon, someone he had known personally and professionally for years. In a matter of minutes, that trust was transferred from Dr. Weldon to Dr.

Purser. Within hours of that introduction, Dr. Purser was performing a lifesaving procedure on Eric's wife.

This is also the trust allowing exponential growth. Because we trust people and they trust us, there is a geometric multiplication of opportunities through the relational networks that are built on the Internet of Trust.

Of course, the most important person the entrepreneur should trust is himself. Eric recalls meeting Harris Rosen, a billionaire hotel and resort owner in Orlando who is widely known for his philanthropy. "I was amazed the first time I met him, not because of his casual, self-effacing manner, but because of where his offices were located," Eric said. "On the drive there, I passed two of his soaring properties and assumed he worked out of the top story of one of those magnificent edifices. Instead, the directions took me to a two-story motor lodge, and finally to a simple motel room. Rosen had lived in that very room, on his first property, for almost seven years as he built and acquired his ever growing empire. Today, the modest room serves as his executive office."

Rosen's story is the stuff of legend in a city enjoying more visitors than anywhere else in America. A rising star in Disney's hospitality sector, Rosen was suddenly fired, not for a breach of ethics or incompetence— he had exceeded all expectations—but because executives didn't think he understood the Disney culture. Without warning, he found himself out of work in the middle of the first oil embargo, which had brought tourism to a standstill, with $1,000 in severance pay.

He found the property where Eric met him and was able to broker a deal with the bank because the owner was over his head financially and knew nothing about the hospitality industry.

Rosen told Eric, "That night, after the closing, I walked into my tiny office by the front desk, closed the door behind me and cried because I believed I had done the dumbest thing I had ever done in my life."

No one thinks it's dumb today. Rosen now owns seven major properties with about 6,500 rooms, including the opulent Shingle Creek Resort, and is debt-free. This doesn't include the $10 million and 20 acres he donated to open the University of Central Florida Rosen College of Hospitality Management, or the kids in the Tangelo Park community where Rosen provides free preschool and full scholarships to all high school graduates for vocational school or college. Or his employees and their children, who enjoy similar benefits after a few years with his company.

One wonders what would have happened to all the people he employs and all the people he impacts had Harris Rosen not trusted himself and kept going when he felt like he was down for the count.

> *If people understand me, I get their attention;*
> *if they trust me, I get their action.*
> —Cavett Roberts

So here are a few trust musts:

1. **Recognize trust is the "X Factor."** So, first trust yourself— that's the foundation of emotional stability. Nearly all entrepreneurs fail at some time, most fail multiple times, but they keep failing forward. They learn, they regroup, and they start again, almost as a daily discipline. The outstanding entrepreneurial ecosystems and the most innovative businesses around the country, and around the world, have a "failure is a part of success" paradigm. The key question we must ask ourselves is: "Do you trust yourself enough to start again (and again) after you've fallen on your face?"

Secondly, trust others and learn to trust through others. Trust is the real currency of business, and it can be traded and extended.

2. **Don't change the rules.** Anyone could beat a great chess master like Bobby Fischer if you could just alter the rules to your advantage. Have you ever been at a sporting event where people's emotions erupted because they felt exceptions were made, or the rules were applied selectively? When our children are young, they may at times push against a rule, but as long as the rule is reasonable and equally enforced, they don't cry foul. They trust you.

3. **Consistency.** This is much like No. 1. The reason you trust your brakes is because they work every time you need them. When they don't, you fix them immediately. That same consistency of behavior is needed in trusting relationships, or someone will want to fix you. Frankly, most of us would rather deal with someone whose values don't completely match ours; but, are completely consistent, rather than someone who at times is a saint and other times a devil.

4. **Honesty and humility.** Sometimes, people don't trust us once they get to know us because we have represented certain capabilities (competencies) that we simply don't possess. Stepping out in new ventures and stepping up is important, even if it is a stretch. But some people have such a desire to please, or to get business, their desire becomes their reality. There are many things we do well, a few things we do great, and a plethora of things we shouldn't even try. Being honest and humble enough to say "We can only do this..." or "We can try, but I can't make guarantees" may cost you some business, but it won't cost you your character.

5. **Distinguish between confidence and cockiness.** You must believe in yourself, but when that confidence is at the expense of others, then you have crossed the line. Confidence doesn't have to be paraded; cockiness feels compelled to extol its own virtues to gain respect, which results in distrust.

CHAPTER 2

Wag More, Bark Less
Relational Priority

*I believe you can get everything in life you want, if you will
just help enough other people get what they want.*
—Zig Ziglar

Few things reveal human need and the unique qualities of dogs like the natural connection between the two species. It is almost without parallel, and there are countless stories demonstrating this relational bond.

Greyfriars Bobby

Back in 1858, a man named John Gray was buried in old Greyfriars Churchyard in Edinburgh, Scotland. Today, his grave is leveled by the eroding march of time, and it is unmarked by any stone. However, that sacred spot was not wholly disregarded and forgotten. Actually, there is a statue that has been erected in the churchyard—not to Gray, but to his dog.

For fourteen years, the dead man's faithful dog, a Skye terrier called Bobby, kept constant vigil and guard over the grave until his own death in 1872. James Brown, who served as curator of the cemetery, remembers Gray's funeral, and the dog was, he says, one of the most conspicuous of the mourners. The grave was closed in the usual fashion, and the next morning Bobby was found lying on the newly made mound.

This development was something the old curator could not permit because there was an order at the gate stating, in clearly legible text, dogs were not permitted. So, Bobby was driven out. But, the next morning he was there again, and for the second time, he was chased away. The third morning was cold and wet, and when the old man saw the faithful animal, in spite of all his efforts, still lying shivering on the grave, Brown took pity on him and gave him some food.

This recognition of his inexplicable devotion gave Bobby the right to make the churchyard his home. From that time until his own death, he never spent a night away from his master's tomb. For those who have been in Scotland, you would think in bad weather the dog would succumb to attempts to keep him indoors, but by cheerless howls he made it known that this intervention was not agreeable to him. Therefore, he was always allowed to have his way and return to his watch. At almost any time during the day, he could be seen in or about the churchyard. No matter how rough the night, nothing could induce him to forsake that hallowed spot.

Baroness Burdett Coutts was so moved by the relational devotion "Greyfriars' Bobby" displayed, his life was commemorated with a statue and fountain unveiled without any ceremony on November 15, 1873, in the churchyard.

It is the inexplicable power of a relational connection that kept Bobby on his vigil and should motivate us in all our entrepreneurial endeavors. Time magazine's Man of the Century, the genius who forever changed the way we viewed time, space, and matter, Albert Einstein, once said: "Strange is our situation here upon Earth. Each of us comes for a short visit, not knowing why; yet, sometimes seeming to divine a purpose. From the standpoint of daily life, however, there is one thing we do know: man is here for the sake of other men."

The Journey, Not the Destination

The life of an entrepreneur is more about the journey than the destination. And in that journey, your success or failure—better yet, whether your life is purposeful or if you simply turn a profit—is usually determined by one simple factor. It is the people you impact and how others impact you.

Companies spend countless hours with high-paid consultants defining values. But unless the entrepreneur and his or her company values people, simply because they are people, an infectious form of narcissism and indifference will spread through the organization like gangrene. All the other lofty values a company articulates will lose substance and support because fundamentally we are human be-ings, not human do-ings.

If the need to be valued and respected for what we accomplish, instead of who we are, wasn't at the core of our being, we wouldn't be so offended when that ideal is violated. Even when people have low self-esteem or a poor self-image, their deepest need and heartfelt desire is for someone to care enough to prove them wrong. As Michael McKinney said, "Encouragement helps people to change their story."

In each of our stories, most of us can trace a point in our life when someone recognized our potential and gave us an opportunity that changed our life's trajectory, even if it was only by a few degrees. And most have an instance when a friend, relative, or colleague reached out and pulled us back; when the gravitational force of failure was dragging

16 | Dogs Don't Bark at Parked Cars™

us into a personal or professional black hole. Even if no such point exists in your life, why not determine, beginning today, you are going to be that someone in another person's life?

From Class Clown to Head of the Class

Jeff, whose lesson in trying to outwit a barking dog was presented earlier, grew into a four-sport athlete in high school. Though he considered himself "marginal at best," he would coach basketball at the collegiate level. Growing up in the rural Florida town of Dade City, he played on baseball teams with Gene Nelson, who went on to play in the Major Leagues. He also grew up with Dade City standout Jim Courier, who would go on to win the Australian and French Opens twice and make it to the finals at Wimbledon and the U.S. Open. This made Jeff very realistic about his own athletic prowess.

In many respects, it was his Pete Rose-ish, "Charlie Hustle" attitude that was Jeff's differentiating quality. "I hated to lose and was just full of high-spirited energy, meaning I was competitive and enthusiastic!" he explained. "There was also some ADHD in there as well." Jeff saw himself as a good student, but certainly nothing extraordinary surrounded by a mom and younger brothers who were Mensa-intelligent.

The real turning point in his life came when his high school English teacher, Scott Johnson, came to him in his junior year and encouraged him to run for student council president.

"At our school, student council president was the most prestigious position in the student body," Jeff recalls. "I told him he was crazy. The last thing I needed was to set myself up for that kind of failure and become an object of derision. I was more the class clown than the class leader."

What Mr. Johnson saw was a young leader who could inspire and motivate others. This teacher gave something to Jeff the vast majority of us have lost or have had shrunk from a lion to a kitten by the time we are juniors in high school. "He believed in me," Jeff said, "and because he believed in me, I started believing in myself."

It's like the often-repeated story the Indian chief used to explain the conflict for supremacy to his son. He said, "Within us, good and evil, faith and fear, are fighting to win, just like two angry dogs." Predictably, his young child asked which of the two dogs would win. The sagacious father replied, "Whichever one you feed."

For Jeff, the faith Mr. Johnson had in him was all it took. "One teacher taking the time to notice and believe in me imparted something that changed my life," he said. Jeff went on to win the election. True to Mr. Johnson's prediction, it was a banner year for the student council. It raised more money and school spirit soared. Jeff led the way in creating new activities and events that are still traditions at the high school today.

But for Jeff, the *coup de grâce* was giving the commencement speech, titled "Crystal Ball" using the lyrics from the song by Styx, at his graduation. To his utter amazement, it culminated with an enthusiastic standing ovation by the entire student body.

High-Tech, High-Touch

Jeff provided a very similar role with Eric Wright. He recalls: "I first met Eric in 2001 as the pastor of my church and thought, 'This guy is so good he needs a larger stage for his message.' Don't get me wrong. I respect the calling, and he was very effective and well-liked. But his potential as a writer and speaker needed to move beyond the confining walls of the church or a strictly religious setting. We went on together to create an even higher calling with platforms where he is now impacting thousands without changing who he is in the slightest. This book is just one of those platforms."

Before you think, "This is all very nice," you need to grasp how important relational skills are to your future, and the impact they have on releasing the potential of others. Brilliant and uber-successful entrepreneurs like Steve Jobs and Elon Musk learned, often painfully, that ancient principle of "You reap what you sow" when it comes to relationships. The maxim from *The Godfather* film that says "It isn't personal, it's just business" never works when you are on the receiving end of that type of business transaction. In that instance, it hurts you to your very core.

John Naisbitt said almost twenty years ago when he first published *Megatrends*, "Whenever a new technology is introduced into society, there must be a counterbalancing human response—that is, high touch—or the technology is rejected. ... We must learn to balance the material wonders of technology with the spiritual demands of our human nature."

No generation is more sensitive to this reality than Millennials because no other generation has used technology so much to make relational connections more direct. They want whatever vocational pursuit they choose to be a meaningful contribution to the rest of society, either directly through what they do or indirectly through the opportunity their job facilitates. Think about Starbucks coffee; it isn't just providing caffeinated drinks, but providing a place for people to meet, do life, and create meaning. Starbucks' mission states: "To inspire and nurture the human spirit—one person, one cup, and one neighborhood at a time."

This is the first generation that is globally connected in a very direct and personal way. We have always been connected, but as Thomas Friedman pointed out in his book *The World is Flat*, the Age of Exploration that began in the 1500s connected the world on a national level, and the Industrial Age connected the world on a corporate level. But the Information Age is connecting the world on a personal level. We can *like, friend,* and *follow* people, brands, and organizations around the globe. Friedman wrote his book a decade ago, only a year after Mark Zuckerberg launched Facebook at Harvard University.

In a culture where people stand in line for the release of the newest technology, the more apps and devices we create, the more important relationships become and the more people are aware of your relational authenticity or lack thereof. It is also important to remember technology can make transactional work easier and more efficient, but it is no substitute for the human connection. In fact, the popularity of technology is rooted in the fact that it is a means of making connection easier, but it is never a substitute for relationships.

An unfortunate consequence of a generation, whose interpersonal skills are fundamentally linked to modern technology, is actual communication skills are eroding almost as fast as handwriting. As Joseph Priestley once said, "The more elaborate our means of communication, the less we communicate."

Is it Glass or Rubber?

What every business executive understands and surveys by leading staffing agencies worldwide confirm is that the No. 1 job skill organizations need is high-quality sales ability. Every starter learns quickly that although you might have the greatest app the world has seen, you need to sell your idea to other technologists, potential partners, employees, and eventually the capital and consumer markets.

There is an old saying, "People love to buy, but they hate to be sold to." It is a paradox that is only resolved when people buy from people they like.

Great salespeople operate out of a relational priority paradigm. A device can help you be more efficient, but it cannot be a substitute for the face-to-face meeting and developing a genuine understanding and concern for someone. In the transactional and relational sales process, only the transactional piece can be successfully completed through the digital environment. The relational element has fundamentally gone unchanged in two-thousand years.

Technology also affords certain behaviors that lie dormant in all of us. It awakens some like a rising full moon to a werewolf. With the autonomy of social media, anyone can become an unaccountable critic or slanderer with seeming impunity and with malignant effect. Virtual abuse and digital retaliation are replacing the uncomfortable, but much more effective and reasonable face-to-face confrontation and dialogue.

Consider online dating or matchmaking sites. The speed and scope of interest and connections made through these platforms is remarkable in efficiently moving through the selection process. However, ultimately it requires a face-to-face personal meeting in order to advance to a level where the relationship has any true or lasting value.

Many managers or business owners believe every employee wants a pay raise. In fact, pay scale is often third or fourth on the employees' wish list. They want to know they are valued and recognized for the good job they do, are contributing to the team, and are important enough to get the time and mentoring of more senior staff.

Someone once described humans as porcupines on a frigid, stormy night. Our need for the warmth of human company drives us closer together, but when we get closer, we tend to stick each other with our defensive quills. Basically, we need each other, and we needle each other.

Fundamentally, a relational priority focuses on what is right about the individual and demonstrates tolerance for weaknesses. A marriage only survives through this formula since there are no perfect human beings. Love emphasizes a person's strengths and extends the same kind of understanding for each individual's weaknesses.

We should all avoid the tendency and convenience of making technology our primary relationship tool. It is meant for sharing of information. Real relationships are built the old-fashioned way; they are the glue holding us together and the oil keeping friction from melting us down. Relationships are also the gas fueling our personal and professional acceleration. As Theodore Roosevelt said, "The most important single ingredient in the formula of success is knowing how to get along with people."

Perhaps you're a fan of Alex Cross, author James Patterson's cerebral sleuth who has been portrayed in movies by both Morgan Freeman and Tyler Perry. But the following is from Patterson's first foray into the romance genre, *Suzanne's Diary for Nicholas*, which was wildly successful. So, you prefer detective mysteries to romance; that's okay. But consider the power of this passage:

> *Imagine life is a game in which you are juggling five balls. The balls are called work, family, health, friends, and character. And you're keeping all of them in the air. But one day, you finally come to understand that work is a rubber ball. If you drop it, it will bounce back. The other four balls—family, health, friends, character—are made of glass. If you drop one of these, it will be irrevocably scuffed, nicked, perhaps even shattered. And once you truly understand the lesson of the five balls, you will have the beginnings of balance in your life.*

This insight is important on multiple levels. One of the essential characteristics of an entrepreneur is the ability to take valiant risks knowing if it doesn't work out another opportunity will present itself. It is like attempting to scale a rock-climbing wall knowing you're securely attached to a harness. Somehow your confidence and daring soar.

The more obvious lesson, of course, is there are things in life that if you drop through some careless act or because of simple neglect, they may not respond like a Nerf ball. Don't worry; we're not here to guilt you or provide some simplistic arrangement of priorities that will resolve what most of us have to juggle on a daily basis. But we would be remiss if we didn't challenge you to look at the relational priorities in your life and realize how fragile they are.

Accept the fact that we have to treat
almost anybody as a volunteer...
—Peter Drucker

1. **Work it.** Like adding wood to a fire, relationships have to be tended. They are like a garden or potted plant you nurture every day, not a jungle or forest that fares better without human involvement. Also, "the soft stuff is always harder than the hard stuff." You must recognize that developing relationships is by far the most challenging human skill.

2. **Fire well.** One of the first rules of business is to hire slow and fire fast. However, that doesn't mean you approach a person's dismissal like a quick-drawing gunslinger. If someone is in the wrong seat on the bus, it is not only crucial to the organization, but to that individual's success, and fulfillment to help that person see it. Thus, it is not a matter of his or her value as a person, but the fit in the organization. Someone might be an NFL Hall of Fame offensive lineman, but you might not want him on your Olympic high hurdles team. Such recognition can change a destiny.

3. **Watch your words.** Are your words *true, kind,* and *necessary*? If so, speak. Words have creative potential. Tell people they are "stupid" enough and they will believe it. Conversely, tell them they are "brilliant" or "creative," and studies demonstrate they will gravitate toward that reality. Though some may balk at this assertion, no one doubts the combustibility of our words. The term "eulogy" comes from Koine Greek: *eu* equals "good" and *logeo* means

"words." It is usually translated as "to bless" or "to speak well of." Unfortunately, our eulogies are usually reserved for funerals—so the blessing and speaking well come too late for the benefit of the person.

4. **Seek to understand before being understood.** Few things reinforce the value of people, or clients, than simply giving them your undivided attention. People only check their watches or cellphones in movies when they are bored and want to be somewhere else. The same is true with a conversation. Interestingly, young children are much more vocal about expressing their consternation at someone's lack of interest, but soon, as they grow older, they learn to camouflage their real feelings.

5. **The whip or the carrot.** Dwight D. Eisenhower, who had to contend with egocentric and driven personalities like George Patton and Bernard Montgomery, observed, "You do not lead by hitting people over the head—that's assault, not leadership." Demeaning, angry leaders are compensating for their lack of leadership skill rather than exercising it—although we recognize even Jesus once had to turn over the tables in the Temple.

CHAPTER 3

You Call that a Dog?
Diversity of Expression

*Everyone has his own specific vocation or mission in
life; everyone must carry out a concrete assignment that
demands fulfillment. Therein he cannot be replaced, nor can
his life be repeated; thus, everyone's task is unique as his
specific opportunity to implement it.*
—Viktor E. Frankl

If we are honest, the dog breeds most people are attracted to are,
in some way, a reflection of our longing to love and be loved, or our
desire for self-expression. The latter is why we don't usually associate
tough guys with toy poodles. Nor is it our impression the typical female
senior citizen will be accompanied by a mastiff, the descendants of
the "molossus," an ancient and ferocious war dog—although modern
Mastiffs are quite congenial.

"When I was young, I had a real identity crisis with our family dog,"
Eric says. "My friends had dogs, just like our family did, but theirs were

German shepherds, black labs, or even beagles and cocker spaniels. We, on the other hand, had a dachshund. I hope I am more enlightened than I was as a nine-year-old, but at that time our slightly overweight 'wiener dog' did nothing for my male groupie status.

"I knew Bitsie—yeah, that name didn't help, either—could hold her own. In fact, she was quite fearless. Her characteristically long, floppy ears had both been shredded by larger dogs whose interest in the smell of her posterior was something she didn't appreciate and resulted in numerous dogfights. Once a bulldog hopped into our canoe, where Bitsie was riding along, and she jumped, grabbing that dog, which towered over her, by the throat and it dropped on its back like it had been hit with a tranquilizer dart.

"I suppose my father must have sensed the mixture of affection and embarrassment I had for our family pet and enlightened me on the reasons for our dachshund's peculiar characteristics. 'The dachshund,' he explained, 'was developed to smell, chase, and flush badgers and other burrow-dwelling animals from their underground dens.' He added dachshunds like Bitsie were often courageous to the point of rashness.

"For those with limited outdoor experience, there is a reason athletic teams from states like Wisconsin call themselves the Badgers—much like Michigan's mascot is the badger's close cousin, the Wolverine. The name dachshund is of German origin and literally means 'badger dog.'

"From that point on, I looked at Bitsie differently and warned owners of larger, more docile breeds: 'Be careful. My dog is designed to take on wolverines. What do you think she'll do if your collie bothers her?'"

The unique qualities people possess usually aren't expressed in physical characteristics, unless you are competing athletically, like Michael Phelps in swimming. People who are incredible leaders, analytical thinkers, brilliant strategists, or great coders come in every gender, race, and physical specification. When we don't see the value in how someone is uniquely designed, it is because we are projecting our own limited basis of evaluation.

In a conversation with Bill Brown, the CEO of Harris Corporation—not long after he had completed the $4.7 billion acquisition of Exelis Corporation, which nearly doubled the size of Harris—he told us his thoughts were on the people factor, not the physical or intellectual property of the company his organization had acquired.

"How you keep and energize people is on my mind a lot," he confided. "I remind our team, we are never at a shortage of great ideas or of things to fix or things to do, but there is always a shortage of people to go and do it. Our capacity constraint is always people, and the broader your base of inclusion, the more effective your results will be.

"Our company has been around for 120 years, and I have only been here four. My predecessors and I, at the CEO level, are just a blink in time. You have to ask, 'What does a leader leave behind?' The answer is talent. People are the legacy. There are a myriad of essential things we can and do focus on, but what makes an organization great is the quality of the people."

Being able to recognize, attract, and deploy people where they are fulfilled and effective is the greatest secret and challenge to leadership success. That is only achieved by understanding and utilizing people in a way that matches their makeup.

There is a saying in architecture "form follows function." In other words, the form of the building follows the function of the building's design. A factory where automobiles are built has a different form than a high-rise designed for office personnel; the form follows the function.

With people, the exact opposite is true. Our function or vocation, where we are most successful and most fulfilled, follows how we are made or formed. People with average or above-average intelligence can usually learn the roles and responsibilities of just about any particular job. However, some will flourish in a particular role like teaching elementary school, performing audits, or designing apps, while for others, working in one of these jobs would be like having a tooth extracted.

Lessons from Nature

Nature can teach us most of the real lessons of life if we just pay attention. Celebrating uniqueness is certainly one of those messages.

In nature, animals are uniquely different, and uniqueness gives them a distinct advantage in their respective environments. Have you ever seen an eagle trying to run, or an ostrich fly? The dolphin is comfortable in the water, but don't ask it to roam the savanna, or ask a lion to swim the Atlantic. In the woods, deer have a keen sense of smell, while turkeys possess extraordinary sight. Both traits serve as vital defense mechanisms.

This diversity of expression is equally true in humans. Although most people tend to notice and focus on external qualities like color, height, and accent, if you pay attention, the real diversity is as unique and apparent in people as it is in the animal kingdom. Some are meticulous and precise, while others are carefree and spontaneous. Some enjoy leading the way; others enjoy supporting behind the scenes.

Great collaborations are all built around this principle. Rich DeVos was one of his generation's most celebrated entrepreneurial sales leaders, while his business partner Jay Van Andel managed their operations. Together, they made Amway Corporation one of America's great success stories. One wonders if there would have been a Steve Jobs without Steve Wozniak, or would we know who Steve Wozniak was without Jobs?

Perhaps the most outstanding example was Richard Rodgers and Oscar Hammerstein II, usually referred to as Rodgers and Hammerstein. In many ways, they created the "golden age" of musical theatre, with Rodgers composing the music and Hammerstein writing the lyrics. Their work included *Oklahoma!, Carousel, South Pacific, The King and I,* and *The Sound of Music.*

The diversity of expression from individual to individual is what makes the world work; yet, society tends to seek conformity. Though we all see the need for unified standards of character, this often carries over into how we want or expect everyone to think and express themselves.

For instance, we all understand the importance of STEM (science, technology, engineering, and math) in our educational system. It is an essential ingredient for any country or individual to maintain global competitiveness. But recently Dr. Elizabeth Paul, Stetson University's executive vice president and provost, who is also a full professor with tenure in the Department of Psychology, commented to us on the importance of another key component.

She added "arts" to these four disciplines, describing it as "S-T-E-A-M." Paul explained one of the other essentials to our global position is nurturing the ability to think creatively and to release the potential of our imagination, a point both Albert Einstein and Steve Jobs advocated strongly. Einstein once said: *"Imagination is more important than knowledge. For knowledge is limited to all we now know and understand, while imagination embraces the entire world, and all there ever will be to know and understand."*

Our school systems often force conformity, but it's futile to attempt to standardize how we are motivated, what interests us, how long someone can focus on a particular subject, and how we learn. Standardized testing is just what its name indicates—"standardized"—and if we understand the diversity of expression and the uniqueness of individuals, then how can we "standardize" our children?

A standardized measure of knowledge is not a prediction of success. Yet, that is the crown we often place on students.

Today, employers realize someone's Emotional Quotient (EQ) is as valuable as their Intelligence Quotient (IQ). This is why we ask questions like: Can they interact with people, can they read other people's subtler communications, and are they able to determine how to motivate people toward a common goal?

We wonder if some researcher is going to come up with an "Entrepreneurial Quotient" test, or Trep Quotients (TQs). Research shows that the characteristics or ADD in school children are the exact same characteristics of entrepreneurs or your Trep Quotient (TQ) . Did you know "short attention span, impatient, impulsive, distorted sense of time, difficulty in following directions, daydream often, act first without considering consequences, and lack of social graces" are the same traits found in children diagnosed with ADD and adult entrepreneurs? Which then begs the question, "Are we eliminating our future job creators for the sake of conformity, with drugs like Ritalin?"

You Want that with Fries?

Eric was the son of a NASA engineer who was involved in every manned U.S. space launch from Alan Shepard in the first Mercury capsule to the moon landing to the beginning of the Space Shuttle era. The fact that Eric liked to surf and aspired to be an artist wasn't exactly the career path his dad had in mind. Of course, Michelangelo's father, who owned a stone quarry, wasn't thrilled with the idea that his son wanted to carve stone more than he wanted to sell it, either. But what would the world be like if Michelangelo, who painted the Sistine Chapel and carved the Pieta, the Moses, and the David, had decided to go into sales instead of being one of the greatest artists of all time?

On the other hand, what if Zig Ziglar, one of the most formidable sales personalities of his generation, had been forced by his parents to be an artist? Ack!

Eric recalled, "The fact that I didn't have phenomenal aptitude in math or a real interest in the subject—mind you, I was in the 90th percentile—wasn't something that went over really well. Then, when I decided to switch from a career path in art and design to being a pastor, well, it took a long time for Dad to come around.

"I still remember I was almost fifty and he was well into his eighties. We were chatting on our porch with my wife Susan and my mom, and he turned to me and said, 'I'd like to tell you something.' I had no idea what he was going to say. But if he ever prefaced what he wanted to say with something like that, I listened up. 'Son,' he seemed to happily admit, 'I could never have done what you've accomplished. You're an incredible speaker and writer, you've built these churches that have made a huge impact. I just want you to know how proud I am of what you have done.'

"I looked at my wife, and she was crying. In 25 years, he had never said anything like that to me. Though it took him awhile, he finally understood celebrating the diversity of expression."

Business psychologists and strategists emphasize surrounding yourself with personalities that differ from and balance your own. There are hundreds of books and seminars available to examine different ways to help identify and properly utilize different personalities. The DISC model is one of the most commonly used to separate people into quadrants of their highest tendency:

D — Driven, Dominant, Demanding, Decisive
I — Interactive, Inspiring, Impressionable, Influential
S — Steady, Supportive, Stable, Sweet
C — Cautious, Conscientious, Calculating, Competent

This type of analysis can be helpful or destructive depending on how the information is used. The key to *diversity of expression* is truly accepting and respecting the other individual's unique tendencies and position. Tolerance is not arguing with another person over differences of thought; tolerance is the ability to hear and respect another's position while not necessarily being swayed to change your position.

We believe that by valuing and affirming these differences, we give opportunity for everyone in an organization to have a significant place and to make a significant contribution.

Nowhere is the importance of diversity seen like in the potato. Yep, what some refer to as spuds. Though the European monarchs were longing for the gold and silver that ships were bringing back from their recent discoveries in the New World, perhaps the import having the most far-reaching impact on their civilization was the humble potato.

At a time when the poor struggled to find enough caloric intake to keep them alive, the potato was a godsend. It grew fast in relatively poor soil, it could be prepared in numerous ways, and once Europeans overcame their initial reluctance, it became a staple for rich and poor alike. Today, it is the second-most-widely consumed staple crop in the world.

It was first domesticated in South America, in the Andean highlands between Peru and Bolivia, more than 10,000 years ago. The native people developed many varieties; so, they had a potato crop that survived regardless of weather conditions including drought, heavy rains, and extreme cold or heat. The Europeans, particularly the Irish, chose to grow only one type of potato for its size and taste. When Ireland experienced torrential rains in back-to-back growing seasons, the impact was devastating beyond imagination.

Diversity is what adds that same element to a culture; like it does to your personal financial portfolio. One of the strengths the United States has is the ability to attract people from so many cultures and to borrow from their influence, while preserving a unified national identity.

Even the Bible, 2,000 years ago, points to this important principle:

Suppose the foot says, "I am not a hand. So, I don't belong to the body." By saying this, it cannot stop being part of the body. And suppose the ear says, "I am not an eye. So, I don't belong to the body." By saying this, it cannot stop being part of the body. If the whole body were an eye, how could it hear? If the whole body were an ear, how could it smell? God has placed each part in the body just as He wanted it to be. If all the parts were the same, how could there be a body?
—I Corinthians 12:15-17

• • • • • • • **DOG BONES:** • • • • • • •

Do's and Don'ts if You're Desiring Diversity:

1. **Think like a coach.** Coaches think about the team and realize it takes players with many different skill sets to be effective and to win. Players also want to win, but they focus on their own role and their own skills, whereas coaches have to believe in their players, so the players will believe in themselves. The coach's biggest challenge, though, is to build a team while developing the players, especially with exceptionally gifted athletes who are often weaned on the narcissism of talent instead of the responsibility of character. You must always recognize the uniqueness of the individuals you lead while keeping them focused on a common goal.

2. **Find the sweet spot.** If you are looking for a "working dog," whether that is to track escaped convicts or to point to a covey of quail, you select a breed having the instincts that fit the task. With people, you have to do the same thing. We talked to a local tech entrepreneur, who is very active

in the start-up community, and he candidly admitted most of his programmers weren't interested in learning about entrepreneurialism and business start-up. "They just want to write code," he said. Remember, with people their function follows their form. Our challenge is to help people find where they fit best.

3. **Give room and opportunities for "ah-ha."** We all want to help people find the right seat on the bus or their career sweet spot. However, we have to be careful not to assume we will identify the people who might have an entrepreneurial aptitude or determine the likelihood individuals might evolve into certain roles. We have met medical doctors who were more excited about building a business or moving into a leadership role than they were diagnosing or treating patients, and that's fine, or aerospace engineers who opened craft breweries, go figure! As a business scales, give opportunities to succeed and to safely fail (meaning mistakes and risk-taking are not only tolerated but encouraged), because failure should be a part of an organization's culture.

4. **Realize racism isn't just about race.** What an attitude or paradigm of racism actually reflects is the tendency to prejudge a group of people based on limited knowledge or experience or simply because they are different. Women who have a bad experience with one or two men can indict an entire gender, or men can do the same thing with women, mainly because the genders often see the world and respond to it differently. There are religious racists, political racists, gender racists, even musical and sports racists, and of course ethnic racists. If you want to succeed, you have to look past narrow generalizations or believing

because some act a certain way, all do. Also, you have to realize the way you see things is not without bias.

5. **Look for the gold, not the dirt.** They say miners have to sift through tons and tons of dirt to find an ounce of gold. But they are willing to sift because the gold is there. We have to view people the same way. Yes, there is always dirt. There are always human foibles and inconsistencies, which you'll inevitably find if you look for them. But the gold is also there, waiting to be discovered and celebrated.

CHAPTER 4

Running Without a Leash
Influence, Not Imposition

If your actions inspire others to dream more, do more, and
become more, you are a leader.
—John Quincy Adams

Though very capable dog trainers and consultants abound, few have risen to superstar status like Cesar Millan, known as *The Dog Whisperer*, who is also the author of three *New York Times* bestsellers.

Sometimes Millan's methodologies have drawn criticism, but he has probably done more to help the average dog owner understand the behavior of their pet than anyone else. At one time, *The Wall Street Journal* said he was recognizable by half of American consumers when he was at the height of his popularity.

A Mexican-American self-taught dog behaviorist, he is widely known for his television series, broadcast in more than 80 countries worldwide from 2004 to 2012. Millan grew up in the city of Culiacan, Mexico, but the place where his interest in dogs was awakened was his grandfather's ranch. He was mesmerized by the wild dogs on the property. His passion and the time he spent with the dogs caused locals to refer to him as *el perrero*, meaning "the dog boy."

By the time he was in his teens, Millan's interest in movies featuring canine stars like Lassie brought him to Los Angeles. He aspired to be a Hollywood animal trainer. Instead, he ended up working for a dog groomer, and then a limo company before opening the now iconic Dog Psychology Center, which was his springboard to fame.

Millan's techniques focus on handling a dog with what he describes as "calm assertive energy," using his methods to establish his client's role as "a calm assertive pack leader." He believes dogs have three primary needs: exercise, discipline, and affection—in that order. Therefore, if the owner meets these needs, the dog is happy and compliant. Millan contends American dog owners lavish affection on their dogs, but fail to provide enough opportunity for exercise and give them even less constructive discipline. (We really are talking about dogs here, not children).

His secret is not trying to get dogs to behave like four-legged people; in fact, training dogs is only half of the equation. He is actually training the dog owners to think and understand how and why dogs act the way they do. The result is aggressive dogs, or dogs with behavioral problems, as multifaceted as their human counterparts, become happy, playful, and compliant pets.

What Millan is in the dog world is what the most effective and productive leaders are in the business world. They learn how to, as Jim Collins says, "Get the right people on the bus and the wrong people off the bus."

They aren't imposing something on people; they provide a platform and setting where partners and employees are given the opportunity to do what they love. Like Michelangelo, who once said he didn't carve a marble block into a statue, rather he liberated the figure that was already there imprisoned in the stone, leaders are able to release what people long to be and are willing to work tirelessly to attain.

It is like that amazing scene in *The Jerk*. Steve Martin, whose comic genius first went viral in the 1970s on "Saturday Night Live," made it to the big screen in this film. Martin's character, Navin R. Johnson, is the adopted white son of African-American sharecroppers who grows to adulthood seemingly unaware he has no biological connection with his family. The real differentiator is not his obvious skin color, but his utter lack of rhythm when his adopted family plays soulful blues music.

One night all that changes. He hears a Roger Wolfe Kahn Orchestra song called "Crazy Rhythm" on the radio, and he spontaneously breaks into dance. Suddenly, the klutz who couldn't snap his fingers on beat was making moves like Fred Astaire.

The truth behind the absurdity is that we all have a song or a dance deep inside us longing to be released. Not to belabor the film analogies, but as Will Smith said to Matt Damon in *The Legend of Bagger Vance*, "Yep ... inside each and every one of us is one true authentic swing ... somethin' we was born with ... somethin' that's ours and ours alone ... somethin' that can't be taught to ya or learned. ... Over time the world can rob us of that swing ... it get buried inside us under all our wouldas and couldas and shouldas. ... Some folk even forget what their swing was like. ..."

The essence of leadership is not only finding that song, dance, or swing for ourselves, it's realizing leadership isn't motivating people to do what the leader wants them to do, but aligning them to do what they're made to do. In other words, helping them find their own song, not simply singing backup for the leader. That is the difference between influence and imposition.

Put Me In, Coach!

You may be thinking, wait, I can't spend my life creating stages where others sing or dance; I have to pursue my vision. Yes, you do, but even when people are singing in your choir, they should be there because they love singing. If they don't, it will show.

Truly remarkable leaders inspire people by identifying the greater love or purpose that motivates them; so, that they want to do things they may not love doing. My kids never liked picking up their room, but if I said, "Hurry up and clean your room, we are going to get ice cream when you're finished," or even better, "We're going to Disney World," it was amazing how enthusiastic they became.

How do officers leading soldiers into the horrors of combat inspire them, especially when the bravado of enlistment and boot camp wears off? It isn't hatred of the enemy, it is love for your country, and more specifically for your countrymen and women who are fighting right next to you. This is what Viktor Frankl meant when he said, "Life can be pulled by goals just as surely as it can be pushed by drives."

Everyone wants to be on the field of play in life. Great coaches and great leaders realize success comes from identifying where someone's strengths and abilities lie, not in trying to force people to be what they simply are not. There is a difference between being stretched out of your comfort zone and being miscast in a role you simply were never meant to play.

Tom Brady is arguably the most talented and successful quarterback of his era, and Nadamukong Suh is an equally gifted NFL defensive tackle. Imagine for a moment, if for just one game or one quarter, they were forced into each other's roles. The results would be catastrophic. Those two Hall-of-Fame-level players would have their confidence and self-worth shattered, and the team would all be howling, "What is the coach thinking?" Yet in business, it happens all the time.

Effective coaches are the ones who recognize the talent and potential a player already possesses and then work to develop and integrate those abilities into a team. They position a player to maximize his or her skills; while using other players to compensate for any weaknesses.

Therefore, the goal of leadership is not realized by imposing one's will on others, but instead by helping individuals discover, develop, and deploy the creativity and motivation that is already there.

Mind you, the process of discovery, development, and deployment can be challenging because it takes honesty and acknowledging weaknesses as a critical step in unleashing anyone's full talent and capabilities. There is a sense of vulnerability in this process because few people are comfortable facing their weaknesses in the mirror, which is why we often opt for a mask.

Our word "hypocrite" comes from the root word *hypokrisis*, which describes an actor performing on a stage. Some translate it as "under the mask" because Greek actors wore the mask of comedy's smile or tragedy's frown to hide their faces. Unfortunately, we often don a mask on the stage of life, not realizing that predictability and "What you see is what you get" is what people look for in anything they consider reliable or trustworthy. Who wants to walk on a floor that is only a thin veneer, where you will crash through once you take a step?

The process of authenticity and vulnerability begins with the leader first because if we haven't learned to lead ourselves, we can't possibly lead others. As the old adage says: "Leader of one, leader of many; can't lead one, can't lead any."

That starts with self-awareness. Every morning you have to make a point to glimpse in the mirror and do a self-awareness check. The balancing values of humility and confidence must be in place as you start your day, like taking your vitamins or going for a run. People can't follow, nor will they follow an image; either who we are has substance, or it is an easily detectable mirage.

Roots and Wings

Few in our experience embody the concept of roots and wings like our friend Harvey Massey, who built Massey Services into the largest privately owned pest control company in America. Massey likes to reflect on when he started the company and was staying in the Mount Vernon motel in Winter Park, Florida. It was not exactly the five-star accommodations to which Massey had grown accustomed.

Having risen like a meteor to the pinnacle of his industry, he now was facing the greatest challenge of his life. Leaving behind the security and prestige of corporate America with Orkin and Terminix, he was embarking on a journey to build something he could call his own. It was that undeniable *call of the wild* that beckons within certain individuals, the voice that says, "This is what you were meant for."

With an enviable C-suite position in his rearview mirror, Massey was taking over an ailing company and now was $4 million in debt, at a time when he had two children in college and one in high school. It was beyond risky, but he understood the challenge and the principles of turning around an anemic business.

As he finished his dinner in a small Chinese restaurant and put the final touches on the presentation to be given to his service technicians, a week after he closed on the deal to purchase the company, he opened his fortune cookie before leaving for the meeting. Thirty years later, he still carries the laminated message with him. It is a reminder and conveys a kind of wondrous quality. "You will make great gains in any project you undertake, Wed., Feb. 27, 1985."

Massey credits his family and the small community in Louisiana where he grew up for providing him with the examples and many of the life skills that have guided his astonishing career. "When I was young, I read an American Indian proverb that I never forgot," he reflected. "Basically, it said there are two things a family should give to their children: roots and wings. That is what my family provided me, and I, in turn, wanted to provide those same things for my children and for others."

Leaders provide just that—roots, or a sense of purpose and an answer to the all-important "why," as well as the wings that give the "what" and the "how." Massey has supplied both roots and wings to his employees, who number in the thousands.

Massey imparts successful life lessons to all. For instance, he says, "I believe firmly that you hire image and attitude, then train skill. Image is everything. People believe what they see versus what they hear. If a service technician arrives at someone's home looking disheveled, in a dilapidated vehicle, it is unlikely that person will even get in the door. That is the first thing I consider when making a hire. If you don't get the 'look' right, you'll never get the 'act' right."

Or, "You can't manage what you don't know; a leader's first responsibility is to continually gather information. Critics are always out there, but there is one critic you can never ignore: your customers." Then he adds, "People say knowledge is power, but that is only part of the equation. It is what you do with what you know that brings power. In business, you have to know why people buy and why they don't, and you also have to know why they quit or cancel. There never has been a business model that is permanent; you have to be continually informed and responsive…look at Blackberry. Your occupation tells me what you do. But how you do it tells me who you are."

What Kind of Influence?

John Maxwell describes leadership as "influence." In *The 21 Irrefutable Laws of Leadership* he wrote, "If you can't influence people, they will not follow you. And if people won't follow, you are not a leader. That's the Law of Influence." Though there are many components of leadership, not all influence is the kind of leadership we're talking about.

A weakness of Maxwell's definition is that it lacks the clarification of "inspirational influence." It is sort of taken as a given; however, we have come to realize nothing should be left for assumption. The connection between influence and leadership is correct, but it does not mean the end result is positive. Great leadership must provide "inspirational influence" toward a goal that brings value to humankind or has a higher purpose.

Inspirational influence is what brings the best out of others or causes them to become better, and the end goal is a meaningful purpose. Just plain influence does not necessarily mean you are achieving the best from others. In some situations, a leader can be "influential" but the goal is flawed, and the result can be disastrous.

Compare two leaders of the 20th century: Adolf Hitler and Martin Luther King Jr. Both led masses of people and accomplished many things. Both were incredibly gifted motivators. But examine the results. Which one brought value to humankind?

Richard Barrett's definition of leadership is the single best we have come across: "The courageous pursuit of a vision in such a manner that it resonates with the souls of people." That is inspirational influence, which moves people toward a goal of real value! It resonates with the soul, not the head.

In February of 1962, Attorney General Robert F. Kennedy and his wife Ethel were in Japan in preparation for an anticipated visit by his brother, President John F. Kennedy. President Kennedy had won acclaim in the war with Japan as the skipper of PT109 and wanted to be the first American president to visit the country, cementing the peacetime relationship between the former adversaries.

Many in Japan were still understandably hostile and suspicious of their American conquerors, but fanning the flames of hostility was an influence from Soviet Russia and Communist China that few can comprehend today. Robert Kennedy was scheduled to give a speech at the prestigious Waseda University in Tokyo on the second day of his visit; but, was warned by the CIA that agitators would try to disrupt the gathering and was advised not to attend.

Kennedy, however, arrived without any security detail or local police presence (remember this was 1962) to an overcrowded auditorium of thousands of students practically in bedlam. There were 3,500 in the hall that seated 1,500 and another 4,000 stood outside. In addition, the assembly was broadcast live on Japanese television. Shortly after his entry, the Marxists who were spread throughout the crowd started chanting and hurling insults at Kennedy.

Most of the nation watched in horror as the ordinarily polite and dignified Japanese hosts saw their distinguished foreign guest and brother of the U.S. President treated with public contempt. The communists were yelling, "Kennedy go home," and the anti-communists were yelling back. The communist leader, Yuzo Tachiya, wanted to turn the speech into a debate on American foreign policy and persisted in shouting down every attempt Kennedy made to calm and address the crowd.

Finally, RFK said, "There is a gentleman down in the front who evidently disagrees with me. If he will ask a single question, I will try and give an answer. That is the democratic way and the way we should proceed. He is asking a question and is entitled to courtesy." Tachiya took the stage, and then the audience in the hall and across the nation on TV saw Kennedy bow to his heckler and lead him to the microphone, keeping his hand gently on Tachiya's shoulder. Tachiya immediately went into a ten-minute diatribe on a long series of sensitive issues from nuclear war to the Bay of Pigs invasion.

Then, as Kennedy was about to respond, a portion of the auditorium lights went dead, and the public-address system failed. Kennedy, however, realized the TV audio and video transmissions continued. When order was restored, Kennedy spoke to the audience, "We in America believe that we should have divergences of views and that everyone has the right to express themselves. We believe that young people have the right to speak out and give their views and ideas. We believe opposition is important. It's only through a discussion of issues and questions that my country can determine in what direction it should go." Kennedy then explained that this wasn't the case in communist countries.

According to eyewitnesses, Kennedy wasn't ruffled or angry and knew what he wanted to say. The impromptu display of calm eloquence transformed the mood in the auditorium and across the nation. It was influence, not imposition. Soon, to Kennedy's amazement, the school's cheerleader-in-chief took to the stage and led the crowd in song. The disaster proved to be a triumph, and the trip became a historic milestone in Japanese-American relations.

> *Leadership is the courageous pursuit of a vision in such a manner that it resonates with the souls of people.*
> —Richard Barrett

Keys to Liberating Leadership:

1. **Look at how you motivate.** Just as people have different languages that they use to communicate their love— some give, some use affection, some serve, some need words—people are motivated differently as well. One of the challenges of working with Millennials is recognizing that what motivates them is not the same thing that motivates GenXers or Baby Boomers. Making a conscious effort not to try to motivate by using what motivates yourself is where we all have to start. Like dogs—which according to Millan need exercise, discipline, and affection, in that order—

leaders must find what motivates their followers as well. Otherwise, they won't be leaders for long.

2. **Stage addiction.** Some leaders are guilty of what we call "relational or hieratical plagiarism." They steal the ideas or the recognition of those who are following them, to shine the light on themselves. Leaders instead should be like parents cheering in the stands, celebrating their child's successes and feeling their failures, not thinking their child's athletic participation is for or about them. When your followers succeed, you succeed, so be lavish in giving recognition and credit.

3. **Even eagles need a push.** Parents train their children for independence, not a lifetime of dependence. Our followers are the same. Usually, we can only take them so far, and then they will need other opportunities for further success and experience. When people move on or move up, we should take that as a compliment, never as rejection or betrayal. As David McNally explained in his excellent book *Even Eagles Need a Push*, eaglets are pushed out of the security of the nest by their mother to learn to fly.

4. **Are you a thermometer or a thermostat?** Fostering an environment where challenging the status quo or institutional thinking (no matter how small the institution is) should be encouraged, or you are guaranteeing your own obsolescence. Also, truly innovative companies recognize there is no real success without risk, and there is no risk without the possibility of failure; so, failure has to be not only an option; but, part of the norm. The thermometer only monitors the temperature in the room, whereas the thermostat sets the temperature for the room. We want

to produce thermostats; there is already a plethora of thermometers.

5. **Parochial paralysis.** Nothing disturbs our comfort zone like someone we perceive is encroaching on it. We aren't talking about not being competitive; competition is what makes us better. Champions rise to the occasion and recognize competitors cause them to "up my game." So, welcome the new players; they help create a bigger pie, not smaller pieces of the same one.

Harvey L. Massey's 5 Absolute Truths

1. You *never* make too many sales calls.
2. The quality of your service *never* gets too good.
3. You *never* get paid too soon.
4. You *never* make a profit too soon.
5. Your image and attitude *never* gets too good.

CHAPTER 5

The Power of the Pack
The Significance of Synergy

*Synergy is what happens when one plus one equals ten
or a hundred or even a thousand! It's the profound result
when two or more respectful human beings determine to go
beyond their preconceived ideas to meet a great challenge.*
—Stephen Covey

P hilosophers Søren Kierkegaard and Friedrich Nietzsche criticized
what they referred to as "the crowd" (Kierkegaard) and the
"herd instinct" (Nietzsche), and not without reason. People are
sometimes driven to abominable behavior based on the influence or
pressure of a group. However, while pointing out this negative tendency,
they fail to celebrate how positive this characteristic is intended to be.

Though humans can drift toward undesirable group behavior, we
have not only survived, but thrived, because we learned to work together
instead of operating in isolation. Call it a tribe, a team, or a nation, but

together we nurture, train, develop, and protect, as well as interact with other tribes, teams, and nations, resulting in progress and learning from the innovations and discoveries of others.

The United States has a Latin inscription written on its seal, *E Pluribus Unum*. It means simply, *"Out of many one."* We are a nation that is fiercely independent and often contentious in our differences. But our unity forms a bond that turns those differences into strengths. It is symbolized by the Roman fasces, a bundle of rods with an ax blade projecting from the middle that depicts the strength of united power. It adorns the wall of the Chamber of the U.S. House of Representatives. Simply put, one stick is easy to break, but bind the sticks together, and the strength multiplies exponentially.

The animal world is replete with examples of this social behavior, from flocks of birds to schools of fish to prides of lions, but it is the pack nature of dogs that we find especially intriguing. The pack is able to fend off threats from much larger animals and increase its hunting efficiency exponentially.

Nowhere is this pack instinct more evident in demonstrating the power of teamwork than Alaska's famous Iditarod Trail Sled Dog Race, dubbed "The Last Great Race on Earth." The exact measured distance of the race varies from year to year, but officially the northern route is 975 miles (1,569 km) long, and the southern route is 998 miles (1,606 km) long.

James Brooks, who covers the race, described how each dog plays a strategic role in the success of the team and how the dogs' different characteristics promote both individual and collective success.

The *lead dog* is the spearhead of the team. It steers the team, setting the pace for those behind. The lead dog has to excel in intelligence, initiative, and common sense. Regardless of weather conditions, the lead dog must be able to keep to the trail, or the whole team will be lost. There is an obvious takeaway here. You aren't a leader because you like being in front; you are chosen because you possess the right mix of qualities it takes to excel in the position.

Swing dogs (also referred to as *point dogs*) are right behind the leader. They literally swing the sled when the trail curves or turns. In the same way, there are "swing people" who support the leader in such a way that other members of the team follow along. Lisa Van Gemert used this illustration and described swing people on a team as the ones that act as bridges between the leader and the rest of the team.

Positioned right in front of the sled itself are the *wheel dogs*. They're even-tempered and calm. They have to be since the sled is right behind and the team is right in front. Like the Coxswains on a racing boat, they've got to be strong, steady, and trustworthy. These are the ones that help keep the team focused on the goal, even when the pressure is on.

Between the wheelers and the swing dogs are the workhorses of the team. They are the *team dogs*—the dogs that put the strength in the team. This is the heart and soul of any organization. Though they usually don't get the glory or the credit, without this crucial core nothing will be accomplished.

Van Gemert cites a Cambridge University study on this very issue. "They created 120 simulated management teams to make decisions for a fake business. Some of the teams were composed of entirely high IQ people, and others were mixed. The high-IQ teams did worse. Why? They spent too much of their time in competitive debate and academic showmanship. Additionally, they all wanted to do the same thing—the analysis and the counter-analysis—the thinking. No one wanted to do the nitty-gritty planning or tactical, practical stuff. No one wanted to be a team dog."

We have found that in different circumstances people function differently; but in essence, little gets done unless these various elements are present for the team to enjoy the multiplying impact of synergy.

All effective leaders understand this principle. One of our partners is Joseph Duda, the former CEO of A. Duda and Sons, which has vast citrus and cattle holdings, along with supplying 33 percent of the celery Americans consume. He also launched a subsidiary, the Viera Company, a 14,000-acre planned community that used to be the Duda family's ranch, now named Viera and just a few miles from Kennedy Space Center.

His niece, Tracy Duda Chapman, is now the Senior Vice President and General Counsel of the business and CEO of the Viera Company. She once commented on what she looks for in business relationships. "I like business people who are collaborative, who want to make the best decision possible, so they want to hear different perspectives and opinions. Even if you disagree, you make a better, more informed decision when you have the input of others. It is important to know what you don't know and to seek out the advice and knowledge of others."

"The other side of that is being willing to share the credit," she added. "We use the phrase, 'The team made a great decision' or 'solved a challenging problem,' not me. No one is successful on their own. My great-grandfather and his three sons (who founded A. Duda and Sons), when the three brothers were getting married in the 1920s, they discussed staying together or going their separate ways. They decided that together they could be more formidable and effective than they were separate. That is part of our legacy."

Tracy is one member of the fourth generation of the Duda leadership team, an enduring testament to her forebearers' initial insight. The principle that you are more effective working together than you would be separately is still foundational to their organization.

Building on Partnership

We can't overestimate the importance of this in the culture of Central Florida as an economic region. The University of Central Florida, the second-largest university in America, soon to open a new downtown campus in Orlando, is called the "Partnership University," a philosophy advanced by Dr. John Hitt, who has been president of UCF for more than twenty-four years.

Former Florida Governor Jeb Bush described Hitt as one of the most influential men in the region's history, second only to Walt Disney. Partnership and collaboration permeate and define the business culture of the region. Local business leaders all agree this is the "secret sauce" that is facilitating Orlando's extraordinary economic growth in entrepreneurial activity, innovation, and even tourism.

Synergy doesn't just happen, however. Yogi Berra once said, "If you don't know where you're going, you'll end up someplace else," and there's another saying that goes, "If you don't have a target, you'll hit it every time." To build synergy, people have to know where they're going and why. Hitt's "Five Goals" are almost the stuff of legend in the region because they've shaped the university's growth and have been achieved almost beyond even his expectations.

They are:
1. Offer the best undergraduate education available in Florida.
2. Achieve international prominence in key programs of graduate study and research.
3. Provide international focus to our curricula and research programs.
4. Become more inclusive and diverse.
5. Be America's leading partnership university. *(See the Dog Bones at the end of this chapter for Dr. Hitt's principles of achieving a great partnership.)*

The idea of the Five Goals came from a discussion Hitt had with a good friend when he was serving as interim president at the University of Maine. He and a colleague, a retired rear admiral, were talking about goals after they had completed an intensive strategic planning process.

Hitt said, "I'm not sure we have any goals." The flabbergasted former admiral responded, "What do you mean? We have about thirty goals!" and Hitt responded, "That's exactly what I mean."

Explaining, he said, "If a goal is a statement that would consciously guide your behavior and you can't remember it, then that isn't a very functional goal. Who can remember thirty goals? Maybe if you have a disciplined management system, you could do a checklist daily, weekly, or monthly. But for most organizations, when the question 'Where are we going?' comes up, then a short list, which people can remember, debate, and maybe be influenced by serves you much better."

Later his friend came back and showed him the five to eight goals the new president of Ohio State University, Gordon Gee, had made. When Hitt became interim president, he wrote five goals specific to the University of Maine. Soon, he said, "I began hearing them repeated. That gave the idea some priority. When I came to the University of Central Florida, I had five, because I couldn't get it down to three." In his characteristic explanation of the logic of undergirding his methods, he added, "Five to seven is the span of the immediate memory."

He said if he were to add another, it would probably have to do with innovation and self-organizing groups. "I see on our campus innovative initiatives that are being led by the students," much like Facebook was a project Mark Zuckerberg started while he was a student at Harvard. "These young people see something that needs to be done and they self-organize to see it realized. My challenge is, 'How do we seed that type of action for the future?'" One example Hitt cited was a project by professors and students, particularly Albert Manero, to make prosthetic arms at a fraction of the present commercial cost by using robotic and 3D printing technology.

The not-for-profit is called Limbitless, which has been hailed by the likes of Robert Downey Jr., who presented an "Iron Man"-style arm to a seven-year-old fan who was born with a partially developed right arm. It demonstrates the power of this type of thinking.

Another place where Hitt's influence can be felt is a remarkable development in east Orlando called Lake Nona, which is a prototype for the communities of the future. One of the leaders behind this Tavistock Group-led project is Rasesh Thakkar. A part of the Lake Nona project is what has been called "Medical City." Its anchor is UCF's Health Sciences Campus, which includes the university's College of Medicine and Burnett School of Biomedical Sciences. In the future, the campus will also house UCF's College of Nursing and College of Dental Medicine, along with a teaching hospital. It is also the location of Nemours Children's Hospital, a University of Florida Academic and Research Center, Valencia College at Lake Nona, and the Veterans Affairs Medical Center, the nation's largest and newest hospital for veterans.

How does it happen that a vast complex like this one arises from vacant land along with residential and retail development and the headquarters of the U.S. Tennis Association and its training facility, just minutes from one of the busiest airports in the country? Thakkar would immediately give credit to the vision of the owner of Tavistock, Joe Lewis, and the influence of Dr. Hitt at UCF.

"Central Florida is the most collaborative region in the country," Thakkar said. He spoke of a reception for a large company that was considering relocating to Central Florida. The company's top executives mingled with Teresa Jacobs, the mayor of Orange County, where Orlando is located; Buddy Dyer, the mayor of Orlando; Rick Weddle, CEO at the time of the Orlando Economic Development Commission; Jacob Stuart, president of the Central Florida Partnership, which includes the Orlando Regional Chamber of Commerce; and Phil Brown, executive director of Orlando International Airport.

The company representatives, who were from a major metropolitan city, said, "This just doesn't happen where we are from."

Thakkar pointed to Central Florida's cooperative approach—one that enabled Orlando to build four downtown venues during a recession: the Amway Arena, home of the Orlando Magic NBA team; the Dr. Phillips Center for the Performing Arts; the Orlando City Soccer Club; and, a completely remodeled Citrus Bowl stadium, now known as the Camping World Stadium. These projects "put us on the map as the envy of the cities that are of similar size or larger," Thakkar said. Synergy has become a part of the ongoing DNA of the Central Florida region and will perhaps be President Hitt's greatest legacy.

1 + 1 = ?

This calls to mind the old story of two farmers who entered their animals in the horse pulling contest at the state fair. One horse pulled 7,000 pounds, and the other pulled 10,000 pounds. The farmers decided to hitch the horses together and assumed the horses together would pull 17,000 pounds. Much to their amazement, the horses pulled 25,000 pounds together. Synergy is the hidden power that creates a result greater than the sum of its parts.

Thus, 1+1 does not equal 2 in the math of synergy; rather 1+1 can equal exponential growth. Depending on the capacity of the two individuals and the cooperation element, which together is the "X" factor multiplier, 1 + 1 could equal 999 or 9,999.

The Greeks and later the Romans understood this powerful dynamic, and it explains why they were able to conquer the Western world. The phalanx was a rectangular mass military formation, usually composed entirely of heavy infantry armed with spears, pikes, swords, shields, or similar weapons. The distinction was the Greeks and Romans fought as one cohesive, interdependent unit, versus their heroic but unwise adversaries who fought as individual warriors.

Maintaining unity, finding the win-win scenario in conflict resolution, and building a dynamic team approach to success needs to be a core value in any business, organization, or region that is seeking growth and opportunity. Synergy is a universal law in which geometric expansion occurs because the whole is greater than the sum of its parts.

Synergy is when people share a common purpose and a unifying goal; when they are willing to sacrifice some of their independence and most of the credit for the achievement of the "we" instead of the "I." Synergy isn't, however, a union of individuals who all share the same abilities and temperaments. Rather, as most of us have experienced in our marriages, opposites attract.

The authors of this book are a great example of this principle, along with their company and their numerous publications. Jeff Piersall was a basketball coach and made his foray into business in the sales and direct marketing field. Eric Wright started out as an art major and spent twenty-five years as a senior pastor. Eric grew up on Florida's east coast surfing; Jeff grew up in a Florida rural inner-state community full of woods, orange groves, creeks, wildlife, fishing, and hunting, where you had to create your fun because there were no beaches, theme parks, or malls.

Similarly, Michael Rogers recounts a story Steve Jobs told that underscores the outcome of teamwork. Jobs said he had gotten to know a widowed man who was in his eighties and lived on the same street as he did when he was growing up. One day, the older man said to Steve, "Come into my garage, I want to show you something." He pulled out a rock tumbler he had made that consisted of a motor and a coffee can with a little band between them, Jobs recalled.

Then he took him to the backyard, where together they collected some very ordinary and unremarkable small rocks. They put them in a can with a little bit of liquid and some grit powder. The old man then closed the can, turned the motor on, and said, "Come back tomorrow."

Jobs remembered the can making a big racket as the stones went around inside. When he came back the next day, and they opened the can; he was amazed at the beautiful polished stones. "The same common stones that had gone in, through rubbing against each other, creating a little bit of friction, creating a little bit of noise, had come out these beautiful polished rocks," Jobs said. Teams, he concluded, are like these stones.

"Individually we can be average, ordinary, unsubstantial, and even a bit dull and rough," he said. "But through the process of teamwork, we can transform our state." Jobs believed that teams consisting of incredibly talented people who are focused, passionate, and working hard toward a goal often bump up against each other and may even fight and make quite a racket. But by working together, they polish one another, along with their ideas, and create something beautiful as a result.

Savvy leaders understand this principle and surround themselves with like-minded individuals who can bring inspiration and growth beyond the capacity of the individual leader. Almost 100 years ago Napoleon Hill, author of *Think and Grow Rich*, called these "Mastermind Groups." He found that some of the greatest business leaders of all time— Rockefeller, Ford, Vanderbilt, and Carnegie—all used the principle of a small committed group that could challenge, motivate, and encourage each other.

The power of synergy is a universal principle dating back as far as humans have been recording history. Consider the observation God made about Adam in the Garden of Eden: "It's not good for the man to be alone." It's not good for the business or entrepreneurial leader, either.

We gain what we want through the help and support of others. To be agreeable, to be liked, to cooperate—this contributes immeasurably to our success. When we coordinate our efforts with the efforts of others, we speed the way to our goals. Cooperation builds success.
—Wynn Davis

••••••• **DOG BONES:** •••••••

Secrets of Synergy—There is no "I" in TEAM.

1. **Are you a player or a fan?** Only players influence the outcome of the game and truly taste the thrill of victory and the agony of defeat. To truly exercise influence, you have to be in the arena, so stay in the batter's box, not the scorer's box.

2. **Cooperation and collaboration are the oil and gas to the engine of partnerships.** Cooperation is not about who is right, but what is right. Collaboration is like surfing; it looks easy until you try it. If you are going to be a team member, you have to recognize that just as movement in the body is produced because we have opposing muscles, like triceps and biceps that provide motion to our arm, there is a dynamic of give and take along with healthy friction that moves an organization or process forward.

3. **Good may be good enough.** Thanks to Jim Collins, everyone knows that "good" can be the enemy of "great." But synergy sometimes requires you to set aside the ideal outcome you want for a reasonable outcome you can attain. Otherwise, you may get nothing. Our country would not have survived a decade had strong-minded individuals with overarching regional allegiances not been able to find a middle ground where they could work. That is how the game is played.

4. **See the big picture.** Synergy is about winning the game, even if that means you have to hit a sacrifice fly to advance a base runner, versus swinging for the homerun (pardon the baseball analogy). For this to be achieved, it comes down to not who is right, but what is right. Like the Cambridge

University experiment that found it was the smarter teams that got bogged down in intellectual gridlock, we have to keep our eye on the goal and not jockey for position or posture for credit or potential blame.

5. **Limited partnerships.** We have seen what happens when intelligent and motivated people try to merge their visions. Often, it is di-vision, or worse di-vorce. Partnerships are what this chapter deals with, but often the entrepreneur has to understand what he or she is willing to surrender in terms of equity and control when entering a business partnership. Like a marriage, it can be heaven on Earth or hell on Earth. Most of the synergistic successes we have seen come from collaborations that are limited where the circles are overlapping, versus a complete merger with equal control. Someone has to have the authority to make the final decision, and that should be determined in advance.

BONUS:

Dr. John Hitt, the evangelist of partnerships and president of the University of Central Florida, provides five key points to successful partnerships:

1. Define your goal—know your WHY.
2. Identify the potential partners.
3. Be willing to give to get.
4. Be flexible.
5. Be mindful of potential unforeseen benefits.

CHAPTER 6

The Call of the Wild
Prevailing Vision

Every vision is a joke until the first man accomplishes it;
once realized, it becomes commonplace.
—Dr. Robert Goddard, Father of Modern Rocketry

Never in history has more attention been given to the subject of entrepreneurialism than today. Dr. Tom O'Neal leads GrowFL, an organization supporting second-stage growth companies across Florida, and he founded the University of Central Florida Business Incubation Program. Though publicly funded, UCFBIP has generated a $7.95 return on every $1 of investment. O'Neal once told us, "Twenty years ago no one could pronounce 'entrepreneur,' and now it is the subject on everyone's mind," and with good reason.

Jim Clifton, the chairman of Gallup, made some stunning assertions based on his company's global data mining in his new classic *The Coming Jobs War*. One is, "If the image of free enterprise and entrepreneurship is going up among your youth, you will experience job creation. If it is trending down, may God be with you." Let that sink in. If free enterprise and entrepreneurship is trending upward, the job creation conundrum will be solved. If it is trending downward, we're in deep trouble.

Equally amazing, based on his company's research, Clifton goes on to say, "Entrepreneurship is more important than innovation." That almost sounds like heresy! "Supply and demand is backward here: almost all countries, states, and cities have bet everything on innovation. The investments instead should follow rare entrepreneurs versus the worldwide oversupply of innovation. Put another way; it's far better to invest in entrepreneurial people than in great ideas."

But what is entrepreneurialism at its most primal place, if it is not a cry to release the creative aspirations deep inside all of us? If we aren't able to shape the destiny of our nation or community, at least we long to have the freedom to be the "captain of our own fate, the master of our own soul."

Few captured that primal urge like author Jack London in *Call of the Wild*. Not only was it one of the great adventure stories of all time, it also was the first fictional biography of a dog. You probably were assigned to read it in eighth-grade English and did what we did, read the *Cliff Notes*, but it was and is as remarkable as the Shakespeare or Mark Twain we were assigned to read as well.

The story follows the journey of Buck, a large and powerful St. Bernard-Scotch Collie. He lives an enviable life in California's Santa Clara Valley, with his kind master Judge Miller. Even while he's in this fully domesticated environment, the roots of Buck's nature still summon him. "But especially he loved to run in the dim twilight of the summer midnights," the book read, "listening to the subdued and sleepy murmurs of the forest, reading signs and sounds as a man may read a book, and seeking for the mysterious something that called—called, waking or sleeping, at all times, for him to come."

Kidnapped and taken to the Yukon to be a sled dog during the gold rush, Buck hones his survival instincts and gradually severs the ties to domesticity that through abuse and tragedy lose their hold. "Deep in the forest a call was sounding," London's story goes, "and as often as he heard this call, mysteriously thrilling and luring, he felt compelled to turn his back upon the fire and the beaten earth around it, and to plunge into the forest, and on and on, he knew not where or why; nor did he wonder where or why, the call sounding imperiously, deep in the forest."

London goes on to use Buck to describe something we are all seeking: "There is an ecstasy that marks the summit of life, when one is most alive and beyond which life cannot rise. This ecstasy comes to the artist, caught up and out of himself in a sheet of flame; it comes to the soldier, war-mad in a stricken field and refusing quarter; and it came to Buck, leading the pack, sounding the old wolf-cry, straining after the food that was alive and that fled swiftly before him through the moonlight."

We contend that ecstasy, that elation of being fully alive, that freedom, comes to the entrepreneur when he or she pursues a vision.

The Power of 'What' and 'Why'

If you ever wonder about the power of vision, try this experiment: Take a mother, chosen randomly in a major eastern U.S. city, and tell her you have all of her possessions—credit cards, phone, money, keys, car, everything. Then explain that her five-year-old daughter is in Los Angeles and in a matter of hours she will be turned out onto the street. Of course, explain the hypothetical nature of the scenario, as even "hypothetically speaking" you will see a combination of fear and anger sweep over her face. Then pose this question—"If you are not in LA within 24 hours you will never see your daughter again—will you be there?"

The answer every time is "Absolutely YES!"

Then ask "How?" The answer is always; "I don't know, but I will figure it out."

This is the power of "what" can and should be done and the "why," which is always greater than the "how." And vision is always about the what and the why. When the vision is clear, when it is believed, it elevates the soul and opens the world to possibilities. Andy Stanley said, "We value integrity, but we follow clarity." Adding, "Clarity is a magnetic picture of the future."

As we enter an era of hyper-change, visionary leadership has never been more critical. Vision is the constant providing hope, and without hope, we wither like a plant without sun or water. Solomon said, "Without a vision, people perish." Another translation is "Without vision people are unrestrained" or "They are pulled in many directions." Why? Because they are looking for something that provides clarity and purpose.

Some have said Walt Disney told his crew to "build the castle first" when constructing Walt Disney World, knowing that vision would continue to serve as motivation throughout the project. Oftentimes, when people fail to achieve what they want in life, it's because their vision isn't compelling enough.

Most communities are built on the visions of a succession of leaders, which many times span centuries. Even Savannah, Georgia, which General Oglethorpe laid out in the early 1700s, took a score of generations to evolve into the coastal tourist and shipping destination it is today. It is rare when a booming regional economy can be said to be the result of two unique visions, but east central Florida certainly is.

In May of 1961, the same month America launched her first astronaut into space atop a converted Redstone ballistic missile, a young, dynamic President, John F. Kennedy, set an audacious goal before Congress. *"I believe that this nation should commit itself to achieving the goal, before this decade is out, of landing a man on the moon and returning him safely to the Earth."*

The challenge was a fantasy to many. Yet, in another even more famous speech given later at Rice University, he would add, *"It is not surprising that some would have us stay where we are a little longer to rest, to wait. But this country of the United States was not built by those who waited and rested and wished to look behind them. This country was conquered by those who moved forward —and so will space."*

From that bold vision, America inaugurated the Space Age. It also helped to maintain our edge in technology and provided the impetus not only for exploration, but for advances in computer technology, medicine, communications, and things we just take for granted today like GPS, cellphones, advances in plastics and metallurgy, and hundreds of TV channels.

The impact on Central Florida was transformational. A sleepy citrus and tourist-based economy became the site of some of modern man's highest achievements, which in turn spawned high-tech businesses and universities.

The other vision that shaped the region was the dream of the man Andy Warhol claimed was the greatest artist of the 20th century. He was the one who said, "It's kind of fun to do the impossible" and "All our dreams can come true; if we have the courage to pursue them." We speak of Walt Disney. He was more than just the creative genius behind animation; he also invented the modern theme park.

Disney's success with Southern California's Disneyland came with one obvious drawback even Walt did not foresee. The collateral development that would spring up around his amazing creation was a real estate bonanza, which quickly landlocked his expansion plans. So, Disney looked to Florida as a place where he could fulfill the full scope of what land constraints prevented him from doing on the West Coast.

Most have heard of Disney flying over Central Florida in a private aircraft, looking for a place to locate his dream world and seeing the interchange of I-4 and the Florida Turnpike. According to contemporary accounts, he landed in Orlando and began the process of acquiring the 27,443 acres making up Walt Disney World.

Today, Orlando is the most visited destination in the country, as well as the world. In 2015, Orlando broke previous records, hosting 62 million visitors—twice the number that Paris or London enjoy. Orlando has more visitors every day than Atlanta has residents. Disney's vision was the impetus for many other visions, including Universal Studios Florida, Sea World, and Legoland theme parks, and the empires of hotel magnate Harris Rosen.

Making the Dream Come True

The term BHAG or "big hairy audacious goal" has practically been assimilated into our popular vernacular. It is one of the concepts that characterize great people, great companies, and great institutions. These individuals and teams set a vision that is by its nature basically a BHAG (on steroids).

Vision needs to be bigger than and beyond the capabilities of the sum total of the people initially involved. As one writer said, "Vision is a picture of what could be, fueled by a conviction that it should be." That is the only way to inspire people to new heights. Vision will challenge everyone's abilities and imaginations, just like the woman whose child is on the other side of the country or the engineers and scientists who enabled man to walk on the moon.

The key to all vision is leadership, which is the essence of Jim Clifton's point and a principle that all successful venture capitalists live by: You don't invest in great ideas; you invest in the leadership team that can successfully bring the ideas to market. Leaders motivate people, inspiring and instilling courage and sacrifice in them to achieve the impossible. History and experience teach us again and again that people follow leaders and work for managers. An examination of how a leader responds and behaves sheds light on the difference between the two.

Subject	Manager	Leader
Role	Stability	Change
Appeals to	Head	Heart
Culture	Endorses	Shapes
Action	Reactive	Proactive
Risk	Minimizes	Takes
Concern	Doing things right	Doing the right thing
Focus	Managing work	Leading people
Vision	Today	Horizon—long term

Frequently, one of the mistakes made in organizations is to place individuals who at their core are managers in leadership roles. They are so good at managing people that it begins to look like leadership. But eventually the driving vision is achieved, and there is no new place to go. This certainly happened with our space program, and now, almost a half century later, a new generation of space visionaries are charting a fresh course.

According to Webster, vision is *the act or power of anticipating that which will or may come to be.* As you set a vision or begin to follow a visionary, please remember visions usually succeed or fail because people choose one of two intellectual and emotional positions, **faith** or **fear.** Interestingly, the two words have exactly the same definition: *"the things we believe that yet are unseen in our future."* However, one is positive, and one is negative, and the results are extremely different depending upon from which you choose to operate.

Vision accomplishes two primary purposes.

First, vision is what makes your organization distinct; it explains why you exist. Many in businesses or other types of organizations say, in essence, "Hey, let's get together and play some football." But one group shows up with a soccer ball and another with an NFL football. Both synchronized swimming and water polo happen in a pool and involve swimming, but that is where the similarity ends. Vision says, "This is who we are, this is what we do, and most important, this is why we do it." This gives people the opportunity to say, "Yes, that is what I have dreamed of doing" or "That has no appeal to me at all."

Second, vision is the rudder that keeps us on course because we know where we're going. Albert Einstein was once traveling by train, busily preparing a lecture he was to deliver. The conductor walked by and asked him for his ticket. He rummaged through his coat, and the conductor assured the famous scientist it was all right. When the conductor returned, Einstein was on his hands and knees looking under the seat. The conductor interrupted his search saying, "Don't worry, doctor, I know who you are." Einstein responded in exasperation, "I also know who I am; I just don't know where I am going."

Vision also eliminates the need for countless manuals and policies that encumber creativity and initiative. God gave Moses only ten rules, and in the Garden of Eden, they had only one. In the same way, the U.S. Constitution that has guided our country through incredible cultural and technological changes, not to mention a Civil War and two World Wars, could be printed on three double-spaced typed pages. In contrast, the Affordable Care Act signed into law in 2010 is 2,500 single-spaced pages. There are huge multinational organizations that have greatly simplified their decision-making process by clearly defining their vision and their values.

Someone once said, "Vision is a unifying hope that drives us toward our future." Unfortunately, everyone doesn't share your hopes and dreams, so keep in mind these principles developed by Marcia Wieder, founder and CEO of Dream University:

1. **A vision is something you can share with others.** But remember—not all others will be able to see it the way you do. There is a reason some called the first commercially successful steamboat "Fulton's Folly." It wasn't because these detractors thought it would revolutionize transportation forever and make Fulton one of the greatest men of his era. The point is, if you can't articulate your vision simply, concisely, and perhaps most important, memorably; it isn't really a vision; it is just an idea. And although you are excited, that doesn't mean everyone else will be.

2. **A vision is something for which you can design a strategy.** Winning the lottery is not a vision; it is a fantasy because you can't design a strategy for winning the lottery. In fact, doubts that arise about your vision are simply elements you didn't design a strategy to address. There are very few elevators in life, but there are staircases everywhere, so ask, "What are the steps I need to take to realize my vision?" We will enlarge and clarify this in the chapter on *Process Orientation*.

   In the course of pursuing a vision, there is an old adage you have to take into account: "In nature, tension seeks resolution." Like stretching a rubber band, on one hand, there is the pull of your vision and on the other the pull of your current reality. The rubber band will stretch only so far, and then it either breaks or has to move in the direction of one of your hands.

   Like the rubber band, your vision has to move in one of two directions: where you want to go (your vision) or back toward your current reality. The question is: Which is going to prevail? The answer is: To whichever one you are more committed.

The Apollo Saturn V rocket was designed to fly 230,000 miles to the moon and back. In fact, 308 feet or 85 percent of the missile was designed just to get it out of Earth's orbit. If you saw or watched a video of the launch, the rocket just sat on the launchpad for nine seconds before it moved, and almost another ten seconds lapsed before it cleared the gantry. That isn't smoke you see billowing up around the missile; it is steam because they had to flood the pad with water to keep it from melting.

When the spacecraft left Earth's orbit, it was traveling at 25,000 miles an hour, seven miles a second, Mach 32. What most people don't know is for every foot the rocket moved away from the Earth, the pull of the planet's gravity slowed it down. It decelerated to the point where it was moving less than 2,500 miles an hour before the gravitational pull of the moon began acting on it. Amazingly, the Apollo lunar vehicle was only 30,000 miles away from the moon before the force pulling from behind was less than the attraction of what was ahead.

Often that is the way it is with a vision; the forces behind us continue to slow us down and pull us back, until finally the goal, the vision, begins to pull us forward. That's why William Shakespeare said in *The Merchant of Venice*, "If to do were as easy as to know what was good to do, chapels would be cathedrals and poor men's cottages princes' palaces."

There is nothing in a caterpillar that tells you it's going to be a butterfly. Ninety-nine percent of who you are is invisible and untouchable.
—Buckminster Fuller

```
• • • • • • •  DOG BONES:  • • • • • • •
```

1. **Know the end before you begin; otherwise, you are rudderless and pushed by the winds of circumstances.** Ancient Hebrew prophet Habakkuk was told, "Record the vision, inscribe it on tablets, that the one who reads it may run." Similarly, your vision has to be clear to you and easy to communicate; so, it can be equally clear to others, if you want people to run with you and run to you. Dr. Deborah Crown, the Dean of Rollins College Crummer Graduate School of Business in Winter Park, Florida, said: "It's important for leaders to be able to articulate a clear vision, along with pathways to that vision. If a leader is able to present a vision but doesn't help provide feasible pathways on how to achieve that vision, the leader's effectiveness can be significantly reduced."

2. **Clarify opposition versus insight.** Often, those pursuing a vision encounter so much resistance from people who just don't like change they grow deaf to what could and should be recognized as constructive criticism and input. We have never been to an early stage venture pitch (such as on the TV show *Shark Tank*) where those listening didn't ask a lot of probing questions and offer a lot of very good but sometimes stinging advice. However, they are there because they are looking for investment opportunities and fundamentally want to help people succeed. This has to be distinguished from those who offer unqualified criticism or are simply citing their experience. Walt Disney's wife, like others, saw amusement parks as a dying industry and believed, "They are dirty and the people nasty." To which Walt Disney replied, "Well mine is not going to be that way."

3. **Define your "why."** It's important to define the problem you
    want to solve or the pain you're endeavoring to alleviate by
    starting your company, but you also have to determine the
    why of your existence in such a way that it resonates with
    partners, employees, and customers. Especially when you're
    trying to reach Millennials, the "why" is more important
    than the "what" you wish to accomplish. As author and
    motivational speaker, Simon Sinek so famously said, "There
    are only two ways to influence human behavior; you can
    manipulate it, or you can inspire it." He also said, "People
    don't buy what you do, they buy why you do it." Without
    knowing the "why," knowing the end before you begin, you
    will be like the sailboat without a rudder, pushed wherever
    the wind blows.

4. **Timing is everything.** Timing is something a person may
    stumble upon. On other occasions, it is the result of a highly
    methodical process. With many highly successful ventures,
    like Mark Zuckerberg's Facebook, it is a combination of
    the two. Birth is an amazing example of the importance of
    timing. If the child is born prematurely, it takes Herculean
    efforts to sustain its life. If it is born late, both the baby
    and the mother can be placed in jeopardy. Unfortunately,
    life doesn't come with painful contractions signaling, "It's
    time!" It is more art than science, and great leaders tend
    to develop a sixth sense about when to charge, when to
    wait, and when to withdraw to fight another day. Gettysburg
    is a vivid historic reminder of what happened with one of
    America's greatest field commanders who thought his
    audacious aggression would always carry the day. Instead,
    it ended up costing him the war.

5. **The distance between the heart and the head is a long journey, but one that should be made frequently. Vision connects the journey successfully.** It is like the story of the old blind man who was sitting on a busy street corner in rush hour begging for money. On a cardboard sign, next to an empty tin cup, he had written: "Blind—Please help." No one was giving him any money. A young advertising writer walked past and saw the blind man with his sign and empty cup, and also saw the many people passing by completely unmoved, let alone stopping to give money. The advertising writer took a thick marker from her pocket, turned the cardboard sheet over, and rewrote the sign, then went on her way. Immediately, people began putting money into the tin cup. After a while, when the cup was overflowing, the blind man asked a stranger to tell him what the sign now said. It said: "It's a beautiful day. You can see it. I cannot."

CHAPTER 7

That Dog Will Hunt
Process Orientation

Quality is not an act; it is a habit.
—Aristotle

No other domesticated animal has been trained to work with humans like dogs. Though running obstacle courses or catching Frisbees or even relieving themselves at the proper time and in an appropriate place are noteworthy feats; the skill, intelligence, and symbiotic relationship between hunting and herding dogs and their masters is nothing short of astonishing.

Watching a dog work a field for quail or pheasant, often in concert with other dogs, while responding to auditory and visual signals of the handler, is art in motion. Although dogs, like people, vary widely in skill and intelligence, training is a key element for both the dog and the hunter.

"My Uncle Jack had a prize bird dog called Becky," Eric Wright recalls. "I would go up to south Alabama, where quail hunting was probably more popular than golf, to hunt with him. On one occasion, we were out with Becky, and she flushed a large covey of quail, and we shot but didn't hit a bird. About thirty minutes later, Becky flushed another nice covey, and again my uncle and I shot but struck out. Then Becky seemed to disappear. This was very uncharacteristic, and both of us called her and then decided to go back to the truck and wait there. When we returned, Becky was sitting in her open kennel in the back of the pickup. Unruffled and without a bit of anxiety, she looked at us like, 'I did my job. If you can't do yours, let's go home.' Which we did."

According to experts, one of the most common mistakes amateur dog trainers make is rushing the learning process. Gary Koehler, a professional retriever trainer, said: "The temptation to get a young dog out in the field as soon as possible can be hard to resist. Born with an innate retrieving drive, the pup is already raring to go. And with hunting season only months away, you may be just as eager to start running retrieving drills.

"Before you jump headlong into field work, however, make sure your dog has mastered the fundamentals of obedience. Be patient and take it slow. There are no shortcuts. To be able to perform advanced tasks, a retriever must first learn to follow basic commands. Repetition and consistency are the only sure ways to build understanding and trust."

The basics for any dog training are the same as the basics for any training, period. You start with the simple and move to the complex.

Rome Wasn't Built in a Day

There is a familiar fable underscoring the importance of being process-oriented: "The Tortoise and the Hare." It has two principal characters: the hyperactive, over-achieving, exceedingly confident hare or rabbit and the persistent, yet uncharismatic and ever-plodding tortoise. As you know, the hubris of the hare caused him to fall asleep, in the midst of a race (we don't need to break down the analogy for you here, it is too obvious) and ultimately caused his humiliating defeat.

It echoes the sentiment leadership author and speaker Mark Sanborn made, "Better to be consistently good, than occasionally great." There is a marked difference between those businesses achieving consistently good outcomes over a prolonged period of time versus those shooting stars that experience occasional, but sometimes short-lived greatness.

For any business, from the Fortune 500 corporation to the start-up that is working out of an urban co-working space, a well-defined, steadily executed and assessed, and continuously improved set of processes is the key. This differentiates between being the comet that creates "wows" as it streaks across the sky, but quickly burns up; and the ever-glistening, enormously larger star that we see every evening.

What is a process? It is what has made the franchise model one of the most phenomenal success stories in the long history of business. Wherever you go in the world, they make McDonald's hamburgers or Kentucky Fried Chicken exactly the same. Their organizations can take someone who knows nothing about the restaurant business, who purchases a franchise, and train them by a meticulous process; and *bingo*, you have a profitable, successful business, regardless of where it's placed, because they also have a time-tested process for determining the best locations.

To put it simply, it is not reinventing the wheel, but approaching every aspect of the business based on the cumulative experience of many who have done the same task, solved the same problem, and made the same product countless times before. As one person put it, "A process is a set of defined tasks needed to complete a given business activity, including who is responsible for completing each step, when, and how they do so." Though it may seem as mundane as a slow turtle, its significance to the success of your business cannot be overstated.

Though he is best known for the impact of his invention the cotton gin, Eli Whitney's greatest impact came when he utilized interchangeable parts and assembly lines to make firearms. He wasn't the first to come up with the idea; it was a French gunsmith Honoré LeBlanc, who promoted the idea of using standardized gun parts. Before this, firearms were made individually by hand; thus, each weapon was custom made and therefore unique, so repairs were not easy. It was fellow gunsmiths who saw LeBlanc's idea as a threat to their corner on the market and shut him down. But Whitney demonstrated how unskilled labor could be a part of a process that built an incredibly complex product, and the Industrial Revolution was born.

The same efficiency should be applied to the processes that run your business. As author and business skills trainer Michael Gerber explains: "We believe that your systems [process] strategy is your business strategy, and the business systems you put in place are your business. This goes back to the idea of the prototype or turn-key business idea—that if you do it right, your business will run itself, systematically and predictably."

In our highly competitive world, where soon products will be delivered to our doorstep by drones and where the tide of offshoring and onshoring goes in and out, processes provide a competitive advantage. With well-defined processes, a company is able to evaluate its strengths and weaknesses and identify where they can be improved. Without this analytical tool, a company is essentially flying blind and reacting rather than being proactive.

Processes provide the means for you to not only deliver consistent customer service; and therefore, customer satisfaction and loyalty, but also to evaluate and improve your products. This doesn't create rigidity. Instead, it enables a company to be nimble and responsive in an ever-changing market, because companies know what they are doing right and can make agile course corrections when they are not.

FINFROCK, a third-generation design-builder based in Apopka, Florida, looked at how buildings were constructed and asked: "Why is each building essentially made from scratch and with so many changes during the construction process? What if we designed and produced buildings using a factory-like system, similar to the way they make cars, and delivered the precision-made pieces to the construction site for assembly?"

The result is a sophisticated precision product that is a market disruptor. The entire structure can be produced in a more economical, efficient, effective, timely fashion and with no change orders. FINFROCK, like none of its competitors, has differentiated itself by becoming a technology-driven company that delivers multi-story commercial buildings and parking structures as a product rather than as a series of services.

It is processes that ensure employee engagement, from the newest hire to the dependable veteran. In essence, processes are the guiding force that train, direct, and evaluate performance and productivity, minimizing the interference of human foibles and personality. The bottom line is— and all business is about the bottom line, or you won't be in business long—processes drive profitability. They point out duplication of effort, and they have a multiplying effect on every endeavor because success in one place can be replicated and used elsewhere.

Processes are the blocking and tackling of the business world, the basics, and here is an important secret or observation. Some individuals are more oriented, we would go so far as to call them gifted, in identifying and implementing processes than others. Typically, this is not the serial entrepreneur's strong suit. He or she is usually working on the next thing before the assembly line is even finished for the last great idea.

Hit the Road Jack

Understanding the importance of the process and processes themselves is essential for the entrepreneur. However, sometimes we like to skip the steps and get to the finish. It is a common phenomenon.

Perhaps you share the sentiment that there are few things more irritating than going into a convenience store to pay for gas or to get a cup of coffee, only to have to wait behind a half-dozen people who have lined up to buy lottery tickets. The desire to reach for that *impossible dream* is something everyone understands. But it is amazing how much time and expense is wasted hoping the ping-pong balls will bring the right combination of numbers. This is the very essence of an impossible dream. All the while, the very practical, methodical, and sometimes laborious steps that are necessary to actually achieve a goal or realize a dream lay like fallow ground waiting to be cultivated.

We aren't averse to luck. Napoleon was once asked what he looked for in a general. He replied, "Luck; I like field commanders who are lucky!" Nevertheless, those who seem to make the most headway in moving dreams to reality are those who see life as a process they persist in, a journey they take step by step, rather than a single event. Of course, events do happen, hopefully very fortuitous events—you meet that right person, circumstances open windows of opportunity, you make a strategic decision or come up with the revolutionary idea that causes the dominoes to start falling. In each case, however, the event is usually the first step in a new and ongoing process.

This myth of the lucky draw versus persistence in working the plan is growing in our culture like a malignancy. To those who take a closer look, the only people who seem to be realizing their dreams in that illusionary world are the ones who operate the lotteries or own the casinos, not those who visit them in hopes of winning.

Which is why the story of "Jack and the Beanstalk" is somewhat of a conundrum. Most fables have an ethical point—an enduring lesson that is cleverly woven into a memorable yarn. Jack's bio continues to be passed along generation after generation. Do you remember the basic characters and plot?

Jack is described as a "lazy boy" growing up in a single-parent household. His hard-working mother is desperately trying to keep things afloat, but Jack is more like the ballast than a bailer on this sinking ship. To ensure they make it through the economic downturn of winter, she decides to liquidate her only asset, a cow. With the proceeds, she plans to invest in provisions to see them through the lean months, in hopes of new opportunities come spring. To whom does she entrust the critical responsibility of managing this transaction? The same kid who sleeps until noon every day. Maybe there is more dysfunction here than we realize?

Anyway, Jack sets out to market and meets the storybook version of Bernie Madoff. This wily trader has a spectacular offer that is far superior to life-preserving supplies for winter—"magic beans." Plus, they are on special, that day only, for the very reasonable price of one cow.

Jack returns home as triumphant as an Enron executive in the late 1990s, explaining to his mom that her troubles are over. When she inquires where the provisions are, he explains the windfall that fell into his lap in the form of magic beans. Rightfully infuriated, she sends him to bed, while she sinks into a panic attack, but not before she pitches the seeds out the window.

Here is where the story really tracks off the charts. Jack, uncharacteristically, rises early, only to find the seeds have grown into a giant beanstalk. He doesn't think, "Giant beanstalk; therefore, giant beans and giant bean crop." That would be too practical. Instead, he sees it as a recreational outlet for his wanderlust and begins to climb. He gets to the top, where he finds a castle and a giant whose fortune is based on a goose that lays golden eggs. In a rare moment of inspiration that would make Karl Marx proud, Jack decides that this is the answer to his mother's economic problems and his own aversion to work.

Jack, using some twisted moral formula, steals the goose and begins climbing down the stalk, only to be pursued by a greedy capitalist, the giant. So, what does Jack do to free himself from the long arm of his pursuer and years tied up in litigation? In a step right out of the pages of Machiavelli, he cuts down the beanstalk and murders the giant. He must have paid off the local homicide detectives with golden eggs because it is hard to hide a giant's body. But the story ends with, "And they lived happily ever after."

What's wrong with this picture?

Like Jack, many people spend their lives and resources looking for the magic beans of a transforming event, rather than engaging in the ongoing process that provides a harvest of lasting success.

Learning from the Master

Understanding the genius of processes and fundamentals was something Jeff Piersall learned from perhaps the best there ever was. He reflected: "It was the spring of 1985, and the guest speaker at the Birmingham-Southern College Basketball banquet, where I was an assistant coach, was the legendary Coach John Wooden from UCLA. Yes, the same John Wooden who was an All-American at Purdue and then went on to be the head coach at UCLA, winning ten national championships, a feat that is still unmatched.

"Coach Wooden was a study in strength of character that night. He had recently lost the love of his life, his wife, Nell. His grief kept him from the Final Four and Basketball Coaches Convention for the first time in his career. Yet, he honored his commitment to come to our little NAIA college basketball banquet, making his first public appearance since Nell's death.

"I was living the dream. It was my first year of collegiate coaching, and now I had the opportunity to meet this living legend. Not only that, but I had heard my grandfather, George Wright, tell frequent stories about his relationship with Coach Wooden when they were competing high school coaches at small schools in northern Kentucky and southern Indiana respectively.

"Grandpa Coach was six-foot-six in an era when the average basketball player was several inches shorter, and he played during a time when there was a center jump after every basket. He was as dominating as any seven-footer today and more competitive. After a distinguished career in education, Grandpa Coach died in 1979.

"When I was a teenager, and Wooden was bigger than life, I took my grandfather's stories with a grain of salt. However, when I finally met Coach Wooden, I summoned up the courage to ask if he remembered George Wright. To my absolute amazement and joy, it took two hours for him to stop talking about my grandfather. The most admired man in my life, who had passed away five years earlier, was being eulogized by the most admired man in the basketball world.

"Coach Wooden and I stayed in touch after that encounter. He sent me an autographed copy of his Pyramid of Success from his book Wooden on Leadership. He was all about the fundamentals, and his speech that night and in subsequent letters made a powerful impact on my life.

"Many years later and long after I left my basketball career, I served as the Little League president in Viera, Florida. I instituted one of Coach Wooden's most important philosophies. He told me, 'Never focus on winning; focus on being your best. You can't control winning, but you can control being your best.' Our league banned the use of the word "win" when talking to youth players.

"In those days, the teams from the Viera-Suntree Little League were always the teams everybody wanted to play because we usually lost.

However, five seasons later, the same Little League program won the district title for every single all-star girls and boys in every age division from nine-ten to seniors, eight for eight, and several went on to the state finals, in arguably the most competitive state for baseball. These teams went from perennial losers to champions. Not one coach ever talked about winning; it was the result of focusing on those kids to be their best.

"It changed the attitude and the culture of the community—and to this day the young kids from that community still believe in themselves, and now nobody wants to play a Viera team. In fact, just a few years ago, one of those teams was one game away from Williamsport—the Little League World Series. All it takes is one small, committed group of people to make a world of difference."

Most people are not aware that the alumni at UCLA were asking for Coach Wooden to be fired prior to his first National Championship season. In spite of all the criticism, he stood his ground for character and the development of young people coming before the winning.

What are the fundamentals of your business? Are you passionately focusing on them every day with a vision for the future? Winning comes from doing the fundamentals better than your competition. So, focus on the fundamentals every single day and be prepared to be your best when your best is needed, and you, too, can achieve competitive greatness.

In the book, *The High Performance Entrepreneur*, Subroto Bagchi includes a chapter titled, "Building a Process-Focused Organization." In that chapter, he shares an insightful story:

"Fuji Xerox was a joint venture between Fuji and Xerox. Fuji Xerox won the legendary Deming Prize for Total Quality Management even before Xerox, the parent company, got the Malcolm Baldridge Award for quality in the U.S.

An executive with the company was giving a presentation on process orientation and why it is the key to building competitive success. When he was fielding questions, someone asked him vainly, "But Michelangelo followed no process!" Unflustered, the expert replied, "First, be Michelangelo. Everyone else must follow a process."

Excellent firms don't believe in excellence—only in constant improvement and constant change.
—Tom Peters

1. **Focus on the fundamental of being your best; it is all you can control.** As Coach Wooden so accurately claims at the top of his pyramid, Competitive Greatness is being your best when your best is needed. The question is, are you your best? Winning is the result of doing things at your best, and if for some reason "your best" results in a scoreboard that shows a loss, then you have not lost; you did your best, the other person or team just happened to be better that day.

2. **You simply cannot win every game; so, if you are focused on an outcome, not the fundamental that creates the outcome, you are chasing an unobtainable result.** We compete because there is a chance to lose, not because we can win. Track and field has to be one of the purest teaching opportunities for this philosophy. You want to win the race, but all you can do is control your time or performance. The only question to ask daily is, "Did my time improve today?" If it did not, then you did not improve, and if you win the race with a poorer time, you should not feel like you won. Conversely, if you lose the race but improved your time,

you'll feel like you won; the other runner just happened to have a better time that day.

3. **It's not the "play," it's the fundamentals.** Watch a youth basketball practice, and you'll see dads spending hours teaching the kids plays. It's foolishness; just go to the game and watch how that play never works and the kids become frustrated. It is no fun at all. Just practice how to shoot, pass, and dribble, the three fundamentals of the game. Here's what Jeff says: "When I coached my son's nine-ten and eleven-twelve-year-old teams, all we did for 90 minutes were drills and play competitive games that made the kids pass, dribble, and shoot. We never practiced a play. Our goal was that every child score during the season; they got the thrill of success. Not only did we accomplish that goal, we also won every game." It's the same in sales—it's who shows up the most wins the most contracts. Are you in front of the prospects? If your salespeople are in the office, they cannot perform for you.

4. **A commitment to consistency creates stability.** Coach Wooden was so emphatic about being your best that he would make players sit and learn how to put on their socks and shoes before their first collegiate practice. Why? Just ask Bill Walton (UCLA three-time NCAA Player of the Year and NBA Hall of Famer) about the experience. It says everything about who Coach Wooden was, is and will be for years to come. The only equipment you have as a basketball player are your socks and shoes. If they are not put on properly, and it creates a blister on your foot, there is no way to perform at your best. Sounds trivial—teaching college kids how to put on their socks and shoes—but it produced results.

5. **What if?** You must always ask "what if" to every process and dream. You are in a consistent process of improvement because life is not an event; only birth and death are events. Life is a process. Don't be like the cooked frog. A young boy conducting a science project discovered if you dropped a bullfrog in a pot of boiling water, it would jump out as soon as it touched the liquid. But he could take that same frog, put him in nice cool water, and turn up the temperature a degree an hour, and the frog would cook to death. Why? We get comfortable and quit asking "what if?" Don't be the frog in the pot; get out!

6. **Don't swallow a camel and choke on a flea.** Keep the main thing the main thing, all the time. Doing the same thing, the same way every day leads to perfection. Practice does not make perfect – perfect practice makes perfection.

CHAPTER 8

Chasing the Stick
Validating Desire

*I believe God made me for a purpose, but He also made me
fast... and when I run I feel His pleasure.*
—Eric Liddell, Chariots of Fire

Have you ever wondered if that robin you see looking for a worm gets as excited and enjoys what it is doing as much as a deer hunter whose pulse starts to rise when a trophy whitetail buck starts making its way toward the tree stand? What about that heron you watch wading in the marsh looking at a fish? Is it experiencing the same elation a bass fisherman feels when a ten-pound largemouth hits the bait? We sort of think so.

One thing is for certain, dogs do. Everyone has seen the much-reproduced series of oil paintings by C.M. Coolidge, commissioned in 1903 to advertise cigars, known as "Dogs Playing Poker," one of which recently sold for a half-million dollars. However, we all know a dog would never succeed at poker. No dog can bluff; its wagging tail would be the tell that gave it away every time.

Okay, you purists are thinking: Dogs can control their excitement—they do it when they point a pheasant, gently hold a quail in their mouth without crushing it, or stay put when you say "sit." Yes, but watch what happens when you pick up the play toy, grab the leash, or throw the ball for a dog that likes to retrieve. It is euphoria. It is, "We just came from behind, in the closing seconds, to win the national championship with a Hail Mary!" level of excitement.

Is there another species that is as expressive in its joy of simply doing what it was made for as a dog? Maybe people?

How would you answer if you were asked, "Where does all human progress begin?" or, "What is it that makes one culture innovative and inventive, while another is stagnant and simply repeats itself generation after generation?"

Though there may be numerous thoughtful responses, one of the clearest is human progress begins with a desire. Where the desire to try, to explore, to create, to develop, to build, to achieve, to be more, even if you fail when you try, is celebrated, those cultures advance. Where the emphasis is on being correct or on winning, but never taking the chance that you might lose, there is stagnation.

Our first steps as children came because we had the desire to walk, and our greatest achievements are produced for the same reason. Think of John Nash, the Nobel Laureate whose story was told in *A Beautiful Mind*. He came up with his prize-winning theory because he was looking for a truly unique mathematical concept. He was consumed with that quest.

Within nearly every person is the desire to make a difference with his or her life. Not merely to buy faster cars or bigger houses, but to fulfill a purpose and to make a mark that lives on beyond us. The passion to succeed, to invent, to make a difference in life is not something anyone should feel guilty about or apologize for; it is the genesis of all of man's achievements.

Psychologist Abraham Maslow made two major contributions to his field. One was his emphasis on the importance of focusing on the positive qualities in people, as opposed to treating them as a "bag of symptoms." Maslow took the novel approach of studying great achievers like Albert Einstein, Eleanor Roosevelt, and Fredrick Douglas instead of the neurotic or mentally ill as the basis of his findings. The second, of course, is Maslow's Hierarchy of Needs, published originally in a 1943 paper titled "A Theory of Human Motivation."

Maslow's theory is often portrayed as a pyramid, and at the bottom, at the widest point, is the first need, which is *physiological*. Even the lowly paramecium has to eat and wants to reproduce. The next is the need for *safety*, to be free of threat to body or psychological harm. Unfortunately, far too many people spend their lives fighting to simply "be safe" and are unable to reach higher potential. Then comes the need for *love* and *belonging*, and after that the need for *esteem* or self-value.

The final level is the need for *self-actualization*, to fulfill the purpose we feel we have in life. For some, that may be an internal spiritual or psychological realization, but for most, it includes deploying our gifts and talents to some meaningful end.

Perhaps this was best expressed in the 1981 Academy Award-winning film "Chariots of Fire." The movie tells the story of two 1924 Olympic gold medalists, Harold Abrahams and Eric Liddell. In the film, Liddell is planning to be a Christian missionary in China and his younger sister fears that the fame and training that will go along with being "The Flying Scotsman" will distract him from his true purpose. In a moving scene where they are intensely discussing the situation, he turns to her, half in exasperation and half in evangelistic zeal, and declares, "I believe God made me for a purpose, but He also made me fast…and when I run I feel His pleasure."

Vocations

"Vocation" is the English word describing our profession. Many don't realize this comes from the Latin word for "voice." Originally, it only applied to those who were "called by God's voice" into ministry. But one insight early Christian reformers brought to light was all honest and uplifting work, from farming to banking, was a calling when done for a higher purpose and with integrity. Therefore, it was a vocation.

When you understand this and your vocational pursuit matches your abilities and your temperament, you experience something very similar to finding a soulmate in the relational sphere. This is why author and career columnist Harvey Mackay is so often quoted as saying, "Find something you love, and you'll never have to work a day in your life."

Sadly, many people's social philosophy or theology makes the pursuit of an entrepreneurial dream or business itself synonymous with being greedy. Eric Wright recalls an experience that drove this home:

"It could easily be described as 'the perfect storm.' Brevard County, Florida, the home of the nation's manned space program and the launch site for the majority of U.S. commercial and governmental satellites, was reeling from the layoffs of more than 7,500 space workers as the Shuttle program came to a close. Local economists estimated the loss of these high-paying jobs would have a three-to-one job loss ripple effect in the community for every employee the program terminated.

"To add insult to injury, the nation was in the middle of the 'Great Recession.' Home prices plummeted and the construction industry, a major factor in the local economy, grounded to a halt. The Brevard County School System, which depends heavily on local property taxes, looked like the disaster film's poster of the small fishing boat trying hopelessly to get over a wave of mythical proportions.

"As editor of two business journals, I was asked, along with a number of community leaders, to briefly address a group of educators and concerned citizens. They were meeting to discuss the impending cutbacks in educational spending, and my subject was the importance of education on business.

"Of all the people called on to speak, I felt my job was the easiest. Education is the talent pipeline keeping all business moving. No emotional appeals or anecdotes were necessary; the facts were all I needed. I opened with a quote from one of the most famous college dropouts in recent history, Bill Gates—and if you are going to drop out of college, Harvard is one of the better ones to drop out of. Gates said, 'I have met many successful people in my industry that didn't finish college; however, I have not met a single one that didn't finish high school.'

"I went on to say, 'When I am asked to do a commencement address at graduations, I like to open with the question, how would you like to win $250,000? Then I explain that according to the most recent data, that is what they will earn in their career over the person who has some high school, or $6,000 more per year. The individual who earns a two-year degree will make $280,000 more than the person with a high school diploma or $7,000 more per year. The one with the baccalaureate degree will earn $650,000 more than the individual with the two-year degree, or roughly $17,000 per year.'

"The response was quite enthusiastic. But later, a politician arose and said, 'The fundamental problem in this current crisis is that there are two political parties in our nation. One of those parties is for the people; the other party is for business!'

"I wanted to respond but was dumbfounded by the equally enthusiastic response to this indictment. My immediate thought was, 'Who do they think have the creativity and courage to start businesses? Androids? They're started by people, who then hire the people who pay the taxes, which fund our schools and pay for our roads and public services. And what are we sending kids to school for, anyway, if it isn't to contribute and compete more successfully in the global marketplace? We're here to discuss a problem, and you're bashing the only solution!'

"I would have spoken up, but thought better. Later I recalled the words of Sir Francis Bacon: 'Truth is a good dog; but always beware of barking too close to the heels of an error, lest you get your brains kicked out.'"

Like Dogs, Like People

We made the point earlier that some people, like our canine counterparts, tend to bark at anyone who is moving. Their loudest howls are usually directed at individuals who are making a difference and separating themselves from the crowd.

Consider these barking dogs:

"It's too far-fetched to even be considered…"
Editor of *Scientific American* in a letter to Robert Goddard about a rocket-accelerated bomb in 1940, four years before the German V-2s hit London.

"The wireless music box has no imaginable commercial value. Who would pay for a message to nobody in particular?"
David Sarnoff's associates in response to his urgings for investment in radio in the 1920s, before he went on to lead RCA and NBC.

"The horse is here to stay; the automobile is only a fad."
The advice of the president of Michigan Savings Bank to Horace Rackham, lawyer for Henry Ford. Rackham ignored the advice and invested $5,000 in Ford stock, which he later sold for $12.5 million.

"Taking the best left-handed pitcher in baseball and converting him into a right-fielder is one of the dumbest things I've ever heard."
Tris Speaker, baseball expert, talking about positioning Babe Ruth as a hitter.

"Heavier-than-air flying machines are impossible."
Lord Kelvin, British mathematician, physicist and engineer.

"The idea that cavalry will be replaced by these iron coaches is absurd. It is a little short of treasonous."
Comment of aide-de-camp to British Army Field Marshal Douglas Haig at a tank demonstration in 1916.

"Everyone acquainted with the subject will recognize it as a conspicuous failure."
Henry Morton, president of the Stevens Institute of Technology on Thomas Edison's light bulb.

"You better learn secretarial work or else get married."
Director of the Blue Book Modeling Agency, advising Marilyn Monroe in 1944.

Though humans love to celebrate achievement, many seem to have a self-appointed role of ensuring the desire to fly doesn't result in the hubris of trying to fly too high. The word "hubris" comes from the mythical Greek character Icarus, who was escaping from exile using wings his father, the master craftsman Daedalus, had fashioned out of feathers and wax. Icarus became intoxicated with the rapture of flight and, ignoring his father's warnings, flew too near the sun, causing his wings to melt and him to plunge to the earth.

Yes, we get that, but the solution is not to stay imprisoned; like Icarus and Daedalus were in the labyrinth that they created, and never fly at all. Freedom and opportunity always come with risks. Many can't handle the power success affords, and others are unable to overcome the pitfalls of failures. It is the role of parents, friends, advisers, and life coaches to help us not get too heady with success or too devastated by setbacks.

The Balcony People

In all of our lives, there are what we'll call *balcony people*. They are the ones who believe in us and tell us what we can do or become. When we fail, they may remind us why we failed, but that we aren't failures. They correct us not by telling us we are "bad," but certain behaviors are inconsistent with who we are and who we desire to be.

The Yaqui Indians in the American Southwest correct their children by saying, "That is not the Yaqui way." In other words, "You aren't being consistent with who you actually are."

Balcony people call us up, they cheer us on, and they affirm the validity of our desires.

The other group we all contend with are the *basement people*, and unfortunately, they can be people who are close to us. They find fault, and they don't celebrate our uniqueness. If we are dolphins, they think we should be running like cheetahs; and if we're cheetahs, they think we should be swimming like dolphins. Perhaps worst of all, they may try to protect us from the disappointment of failure by discouraging us from attempting to succeed.

In koina Greek, there is a word *metanoia*, which is translated to English as "repent." It has two root words, *change* (meta) and *mind* (nous), with the meaning *"change your mind."*

That's what balcony people help us do. When you change your mind, your behavior has to change as well. If you think smoking is cool, you'll smoke. If on the other hand, you are convinced smoking will kill you, you change your mind about how cool it is.

Many times success begins with a change of mind about our desires, our dreams, and our capabilities. Failure, however, isn't based on a failure, but how we perceive ourselves and the miscues that are a part of everyone's life.

Each of us has desires in our heart, and since you are likely to spend over 100,000 hours of your life working, shouldn't those desires and the time you spend working be aligned?

The American Dream 2.0

What we are describing here is what is now often lampooned as "The American Dream," the idea that anyone who is capable and talented can be president, can create a billion-dollar business, or can simply have a meaningful job, get married, buy a house and raise a family. Entrepreneur Bill Rancic put it this way: "The American Dream is still alive out there, and you don't need an Ivy League education or to have millions of dollars in startup money. It can be done with an idea, hard work, and determination."

One of the greatest American dreamers we know, and someone who is a balcony person for us, and we think we are for him, is Sam Pak.

Imagine getting on a plane and traveling to another country at 17 years old, not to tour, but to live. Now imagine describing your language skills in your new home country as "about equivalent to someone who took two years of Spanish in junior high."

Then imagine that same individual turning down the opportunity to go to college as a pre-med student and choosing instead to try his hand at building his own business in the highly competitive field of retail appliances, and in the process making his mark as his company's television spokesperson. Even today, his TV commercials may cause some people to fumble for their remote, but his image is indelibly connected, in the minds of consumers in the region, to quality products at the lowest possible prices… and that is his goal.

Like Lincoln, whose folksy demeanor and down-home humor disguised the greatest political mind in American history, Sam Pak, dressed in a white tee shirt and shorts, declaring in his thick Asian accent, "I love appliances!" is in fact one of Central Florida's savviest entrepreneurs. Pak grew up in post-war South Korea, a far cry from the technical, industrial, and cultural nexus it is today. For Pak's parents, and particularly his mother who worked on an American Army base, the United States was truly the land of opportunity and security.

On his third day in the U.S., Pak became a high school student. "It was pretty tough; I couldn't pronounce people's names and was used to everyone having black hair," he said laughing. "Fortunately, I didn't have any problems in math, so everyone in my class thought I was a genius. Well, except when I had to do a word problem."

Pak started working for his brother-in-law at a local appliance business. Soon he was a warehouse manager, then moved into sales, opened a store in an adjacent city, and eventually became the manager over two stores.

Like all entrepreneurs, Pak faced that crucial crossroad, much like the risky decision to board a jet and fly to the U.S. Would he continue to grow and learn as someone else's employee or would he strike out on his own? It was where he always knew he wanted to go, but now he had to actually make the decision to launch the vessel that would get him there.

Pak and his wife, Eun Bee, who serves as his financial officer, opened their store in what is now a warehouse. "While we were working on the building, getting ready for the opening, the banker who held the inventory for a competitor called me asking for help. He said if I would assist him he would help me get a credit line and let me buy their excess inventory." For Sam, it was an offer sent from heaven. "As a result, we made money the first year," Pak said.

The genius and rapid growth of Appliance Direct came partly from utilizing the most effective advertising medium for their market, but also from solving someone else's problem. Manufacturers' warehouses were filling up with brand new merchandise that had been returned from retailers because they were scratched and dented—it was their nightmare. The products were new and still under warranty, but they couldn't be sold as new. Pak saw this merchandise as a "like-new" low-cost option for consumers. Their problem was Sam's opportunity, a wave he rode for more than a decade until other retailers figured it out.

At one time, their stores averaged over 30,000 square feet; now they are going to smaller stores, with more desirable locations and a better buying experience. Pak explained, "We want people to have an Ace Hardware experience, without the additional Ace Hardware price."

They also reduced the number of brands they carried. "We found that by aligning ourselves with one brand that we think is the best and showing that brand in depth, we became more valuable to both the consumer and the manufacturer; and thus, are able to negotiate the best prices," he said.

Looking ahead, the future of Pak's appliance empire looks bright. Looking back, he proved that the dream of coming to America, working hard, and working smart is still an opportunity unrivaled anywhere in the world. "Whatever you choose to do, do something you enjoy doing, something you want to do, rather than what you have to do," Pak advised. "That is why I consider myself lucky. What I was essentially forced to do was something I found I loved doing…selling appliances."

The will to win, the desire to succeed, the urge to reach your full potential... these are the keys that will unlock the door to personal excellence.
—Confucius

• • • • • • • DOG BONES: • • • • • • •

1. **Make your work your joy and your joy your work.** You are intended to work, so you should be excited about doing it. If not, have the courage to make a change. We have met doctors who became entrepreneurs and executives who became cabinet makers. Life is too short to not love what you do.

2. **Change is inevitable, and personal growth is optional.** You will reach as high as you can stand on the books you have read. The person who can read but chooses not to and the person who cannot read are the same—ignorant. Use every opportunity to gain useful knowledge. Most of us spend hours in our cars. Use that time to listen to audio books. They will do a lot more for you than listening to Top 40 hits.

3. **It isn't about you, but it is up to you.** This maxim underscores personal responsibility, but it also means you don't craft the terms of the relationship, whether it is personal or professional, so that you gain the advantage. A highly successful real estate developer once said, "I always give my clients the first choice on the most opportunistic deals." As a result, his clients trusted him implicitly because they knew they weren't getting the leftovers.

4. **Analysis paralysis.** The perfectionist or the idealist will not take action, or join with others until success is certain when they do. Removing all obstacles, risks, and objections prior to getting started is not possible. You have to know where you want to go and then make it happen. When you drive from Orlando to New York, you know where you are going, but you have no idea how many obstacles and detours you

might have to take along the way. It's the destination—it's the WHY!

CHAPTER 9

I'll Believe It When I Smell It
Life is Both Natural and Spiritual

*Ultimately, man should not ask what
the meaning of his life is, but rather he must
recognize that it is he who is asked.*
—Viktor E. Frankl

P sychologist Paul Ekman has spent his life studying the nuances of facial expressions and how to interpret what they mean. Perhaps you read about his work in Malcolm Gladwell's book *Blink*.

Ekman traveled around the world to places like Brazil, Argentina, and Japan with pictures of men's and women's facial expressions to see how people interpreted their countenances. He even ventured to the remote villages of New Guinea to make sure there wasn't a uniformity based on cultural development.

Regardless of where he went, people universally agreed on what the facial expressions in the pictures meant, such as happy, sad, hurt, or excited. Ekman also demonstrated that we unconsciously interpret hundreds, if not thousands, of facial expressions and their tiny nuances every day.

What is equally amazing is the latest research into dog behavior shows our canine pets, more than any other animals, observe and respond to our facial expressions as well, much like they do to our gestures. Unlike chimpanzees, who have no reason to think humans would help them find food, dogs have learned to follow hand signals almost intuitively.

Reading facial expressions isn't something you have to train your dog to do, any more than you have to train a human baby to do the same thing. It is the first form of communication we use.

Alexandra Horowitz, one of the leading authorities on dog behavior and author of numerous books including *Inside of a Dog: What Dogs See Smell and Know*, wrote this: "One of the most delightful things about dogs is their attention to us: I think of them as near-anthropologists, watching us, observing our movements, noticing our habits. In this way, dogs become very good at reading human behavior: some of the simplest comparative psychology studies of dogs show how readily dogs follow our gaze or our points, for instance. More subtly, dogs can often notice small differences in our behavior: how we get up from the couch when either going to the fridge or readying to go for a walk are different. Dogs notice that."

Ekman's research shows that what we think was "a bad feeling about that guy" may have been an unconscious reading of his expressions. Similarly, often what we believe is subjective "intuition" could actually have a lot more substance than we realize, but we just don't understand it yet.

What is most outstanding and astonishing about dogs is their ability to see what we can't. I don't mean their eyesight, which actually isn't as good as ours. I refer to their incredible sense of smell. According to researchers, a dog's sense of smell overpowers our own by 10,000 to 100,000 times.

"Let's suppose they're just 10,000 times better," says James Walker, former director of the Sensory Research Institute at Florida State University. "If you make the analogy to vision, what you and I can see at a third of a mile, a dog can see more than 3,000 miles away and still see as well."

Put another way; dogs can detect some odors in parts per trillion. Horowitz writes that while we might notice if our coffee has had a teaspoon of sugar added to it, a dog could detect a teaspoon of sugar in a million gallons of water, or two Olympic-sized pools' worth. Another dog specialist compared their ability to "catching a whiff of one rotten apple in two million barrels." To put it another way, dogs using their sense of smell can see what isn't there.

I'll Believe It When I Smell It!

This is why the attitude "I'll believe it when I see it" seems so absurd. There are many things we take for granted that we may never see from protons and electrons to the existence of black holes. Yet, we believe in them because the evidence for their existence is overwhelming. What's more, every day we utilize science and technology, which the vast majority of us can't begin to understand, including the cellphone, the Internet, or the microwave.

Why then is it so difficult to accept that there is more out there than what science can explain? As Hamlet said to his friend, "There are more things in heaven and earth, Horatio, than are dreamt of in your philosophy." Can it be that we, as a species, have become blinded to or been talked out of one of our most significant senses because we don't currently have the means of documenting it in a laboratory? As author and Southern Baptist pastor John Bisagno said, "You go to a doctor whose name you can't pronounce. He gives you a prescription you cannot read. You take it to a pharmacist you have never seen. He gives you medication you do not understand, and yet you take it. That, my friend, is living by faith!"

We think of the physician Ignaz Semmelweis, who discovered the incidence of puerperal fever ("childbed fever") could be drastically cut by the use of hand disinfection in obstetric clinics. The condition, common in mid-nineteenth-century hospitals, was often fatal, with a mortality rate between 10 percent and 35 percent. Semmelweis proposed the practice of washing hands with chlorinated lime solutions in 1847 while working in Vienna General Hospital's First Obstetrical Clinic.

Despite the fact he reduced mortality to below 1 percent, Semmelweis's observations conflicted with the established scientific and medical opinions of the time and his ideas were rejected by the medical community. Literally driven delirious by their obstinance, he was committed to an asylum, where he died at age 47. It would take the discoveries of Joseph Lister and Louis Pasteur to vindicate Semmelweis's convictions.

We believe science, as wondrous as it is, can take us only so far, and when it comes to the most meaningful questions in life, it will forever come up short.

For the sake of full disclosure, the authors are unapologetically Christian. However, we remember one astute observer who said, "There are only two reasons someone isn't a Christian: 1. They have never met a Christian or 2. They have met a Christian."

The last thing we want to do is be "preachy," and we recognize many have a sort of Einsteinian view of a universe: it's too awesome to be a total accident, but also too awesome to be explicable by any human conception of deity. In this we agree; our human imaginations or concepts can't begin to approximate the actual reality.

However, we have found in years of interviewing and working with hundreds of CEOs and entrepreneurs that having a spiritual paradigm is one of the common denominators. Not in 100 percent, but about 90 percent, though few wear it on their sleeves. For these individuals, their spirituality is not something designed to give them comfort at death, but something that gives direction, meaning, and courage in life.

Spirituality is far from being irrelevant, both in their business and public engagement, as well as in their private lives. People who recognize there is something beyond the natural world have an astonishing impact. "If you read history," British novelist C.S. Lewis said, writing to a primarily Christian audience, "you will find that the Christians who did most for the present world were just those who thought most of the next. It is since Christians have largely ceased to think of the other world that they have become so ineffective in this. Aim at heaven and you will get earth 'thrown in'; aim at earth and you will get neither."

In the last century, we witnessed two socio-political philosophies, communism and Nazism, which sought to replace religion with materialistic secularism, and the result was one of the most oppressive and nightmarish periods in human history. In Germany, more than seven million were killed in the Holocaust. As alarming as that number is, it is one-third of the number killed in the Soviet Union—a total which is less than half the number who lost their lives in China. In some places within Southeast Asia, the slaughter continues.

It is amazing how we hear over and over about the repression of the "Dark Ages," and, in some sense, rightfully so. Even the term, however, is a rather condescending label Renaissance historians gave to the era that preceded them. It is like the fathers of the French Revolution calling their era "The Age of Enlightenment." One nineteenth-century political historian wrote, "If rationalism wishes to govern the world without regard to the spiritual needs of the human soul, the French Revolution is there to teach us the consequences of such a blunder."

The Dark Age we have been in with the rise of Islamic fascism and Darwinist socialism should give anyone pause. Are you aware the tenth-leading cause of death in America is suicide? Where we reside, it rises to number three.

It is popular to view people of faith as being culturally lobotomized or just naïve; yet, it was primarily people of faith who worked for the abolition of slavery in the eighteenth and nineteenth centuries and against the segregation that was its legacy. India's civil rights leader Mahatma Gandhi's non-violent approach was more persuasive in challenging the conscience of the British Empire than any armed uprising he may have mounted, because there was a conscience to challenge. It might not have been effective if Gandhi had used this approach with the Marxist regimes in the Soviet Union or the People's Republic of China.

David Aikman, the onetime bureau chief for *Time* magazine in Beijing, wrote about going to hear a lecture by a scholar from the Chinese Academy of Social Sciences while in China. The highly regarded academician said: "One of the things we were asked to look into was what accounted for the success, in fact, the pre-eminence of the West all over the world. We studied everything we could from the historical, political, economic, and cultural perspective. At first, we thought it was because you had more powerful guns than we had. Then we thought it was because you have the best political system. Next, we focused on your economic system. But in the past twenty years, we have realized the heart of your culture has been your religion. That is why the West has been so powerful. The Christian moral foundation of social and cultural life was what made possible the emergence of capitalism and then the successful transition to democratic politics. We don't have any doubt about this."

The Lost Keys

Like a dog's ability to smell someone who walked across a field days ago or to detect drugs submerged in a tank of gas, perhaps our spiritual senses or a confidence that there is more to life than this life can help us find what we are looking for as well.

Eric tells of the dramatic way trusting to find what you can't see became real to him. It happened while he was vacationing with his wife, Susan, and their three sons at his parents' home in Cocoa Beach, Florida. "I borrowed my father's car for the beach day because they were out of town. The sun was beginning to set, and we were packing up to head back to the house. Suddenly, I realized I couldn't find the keys to the car or the house. We meticulously scoured the towels, umbrellas, and beach toys, then started raking the sand with our hands to try and find the keys, without success. As anyone who has been to the ocean knows, you are there for hours, in and out of the water, so the keys could be anywhere. We walked up the beach in both directions without success. I was frustrated and started thinking about how I would get into the house and try to find a spare key. Suddenly, Susan said, "God knows where those keys are, let's ask Him to help us find them."

"Oh please," I thought, but I reluctantly went along and tried to put on a faithful face as our sons looked on with excited anticipation, and Susan made her simple request. We continued looking as the sun began to fade, along with all hope. Then Susan, who was searching along the waterline, turned east and began walking out into the surf. I was outwardly shaking my head and inwardly contemplating the fact she was wasting valuable time we should use to look. Fifteen minutes later, up over her waist in water, she let out an excited yelp! Then she reached down, and in seconds came up, waving her arms with the keys in her hands.

Impossible, right? Yep, that is what I thought. In fact, when I share that story publicly, some people think I'm either lying or delusional, but it happened just as I described it."

The real point is perhaps some of the keys you are looking for in life can be found in the same simple way.

Another reason we included this chapter is the astonishing neuroscience research that is confirming age-old maxims like "It is more blessed to give than to receive." Most kids who hear that in Sunday school think, "That isn't the blessing I'm hoping for Christmas morning," or are inwardly thinking, "Sure."

Yet in the book *A Path Appears,* authors Nicholas Kristof and Sheryl WuDunn cite the latest research to demonstrate that the "happiness boost" you get from your efforts to help others far surpasses what you would get from an equivalent effort to do something for yourself. As one reviewer wrote, "Doing good is a good deal." Not only does it make you feel good by boosting positive brain activity and the release of endorphins, like when you exercise, but it has an incredible return on investment in the impact it can have on others.

Though some supplements seem to enhance brain function, no wonder-drug like NZT in the film *Limitless* with actor Bradley Cooper has been developed. Interestingly, brain scans have found hate and unforgiveness actually have damaging effects to the brain similar to Alzheimer's—again, an ancient principle people are now giving renewed attention to because research is demonstrating its validity.

Another one is fear. Franklin D. Roosevelt, famous for the statement he made as the United States entered WWII, "We have nothing to fear but fear itself," didn't say this because everyone was calm and confident; people were shocked and terrified. Eric's father was at Pearl Harbor on Dec. 7, and his mother lost her first husband, an Army Ranger, in the war. There was plenty to be afraid of.

Remember, fear and faith can both be defined as "believing something that you can't see is going to come to pass." Obviously, one is focused on the negative and one on the positive. But what is the source of a positive faith-filled approach to life?

Though the authors found it by accepting the grace of God in Jesus Christ, we won't quote religious writing. Instead, we'll quote the U.S.

Declaration of Independence. It says, "We hold these truths to be self-evident, that all men are created equal, that they are endowed by their *Creator* with certain inalienable rights. That among these are life, liberty and the pursuit of happiness."

The founders of our country make several amazing assertions here. One is the self-evidence of truth. We intuitively know man is a product of design, not chance, but now, more and more, science also reveals it. Even the "simple cell" could hardly be considered simple. As one biologist said, "Our early view would be to think of a cell like a Chinese sky rocket; now we understand it is more complex than the Space Shuttle."

In addition, we are endowed with rights and goals that, regardless of the situation we began life in, call us toward something more. These aren't given by a benevolent state; nor, can they be rescinded by a maleficent one. They are planted in our soul by our Maker and like a compass, always pointing north, they continually direct us back to the One who placed them there.

Wisdom in a Challenging Age

The other factor is that we are driving pell-mell toward a clash between technology and our ability to rationally utilize it. "Computers will overtake humans with AI [artificial intelligence] at some point," Stephen Hawking, the renowned theoretical physicist and cosmologist, said at the Zeitgeist 2015 conference in London. "When that happens, we need to make sure the computers have goals aligned with ours."

AI refers to the ability of computer systems to think and act free of human involvement or control. Also, to communicate with other computers, with or without human interference, allowing them to perform tasks that normally require human intelligence. To ensure AI stays within our control, Hawking claims, "Our future is a race between the growing power of technology and the wisdom with which we use it."

Spiritual wisdom isn't the ability to see life from some heavenly perspective; none of us have that power. It is, rather, an ability to navigate life using the tools of a focused mind, uncluttered with guilt, anxiety, or unbridled ambition. It supplies a peace that frees us from having to have a concrete answer to every question, like children who trust their parents to know where they are going and to safely get them there, without having to explain how the automobile or GPS works. It provides an access to timeless values that serves as a map and a compass to navigate the often-difficult and unpredictable waters of life.

One of the outcomes of those values is they focus our attention on others. We forget that the first universities, the first public schools, the first hospitals, the first orphanages, even organizations like the International Red Cross, were founded by people of faith because that faith compelled them to address the problems, needs, and opportunities of their fellow man. *Philanthropy* comes from a Greek word meaning to "love mankind," or to fulfill the second half of the Great Commandment to "love your neighbor as yourself," which is, according to Judeo-Christian tradition, the logical outcome of the first half, which is to love God with all your heart, soul, and mind.

The number of people who with modest means offer only their time and effort, or those with tremendous resources who have dedicated a major portion of their wealth to help the helpless, we can't begin to count. Are all who do this people of faith? No, but if they are people of faith, we almost expect it. Like Ben Hoyer, who founded Credo Coffee in downtown Orlando, which gives its profits to enhance the quality of life in the region and for the coffee growers and harvesters who are his suppliers. His personal creed is, "Life is worth living, so I refuse to merely exist. I will pursue a life of meaning and purpose, joy, and fulfillment. The world is not yet as it should be, neither is my city, neither am I. So, I reject apathy and despair believing I can make an impact for good and that I am not alone."

Two outstanding examples of this type of conviction are Steve Hogan, who is the CEO of Florida Citrus Sports, which manages the 68,000-seat stadium in downtown Orlando. It is home of preseason NFL and season opening NCAA football games, several national bowl games, and a host of events, from international soccer matches to concerts to monster truck rallies. But one thing always bothered Hogan: The stadium was in one of the most blighted areas of the city.

The other is Tom Sittema, the CEO of CNL, a multibillion-dollar real estate investment firm. Hogan invited Sittema and his wife to a bowl game because they had lived in the community for more than a year but had never been to a game. As they were driving west from his offices on a top floor of one of CNL's downtown high rises, he noticed the closer he got to the stadium, the more depressed and run-down the neighborhood became.

Then came that defining moment for Sittema. As he took in the environment surrounding the stadium, he glanced up in his rearview mirror and saw the towers of CNL and the majestic skyline of Orlando, just east of Interstate 4. The shock almost caused him to hit his brakes. He was confronted with the world he lived and worked in, juxtaposed against the neighborhoods he didn't know existed, but could actually be seen from his office towers.

The image was inescapable. When he shared the experience with Hogan, he saw a passion and determination about the neighborhood that seemed to exceed his enthusiasm for the fabulous sports venue. Hogan shared with Sittema that he had been working on this very issue since he took the helm at Florida Citrus Sports.

Unlike many who would simply, a) place the experience in the denial file; b) delve into the problem, but be overcome by the challenges of systemic poverty and make a mental U-turn; or c) salve their conscience by just writing a check, Sittema, Hogan, and others like them spent months studying the problem like businesspeople, who make their living solving problems. Together, they began working with community leaders to design a fifteen- to twenty-year road map toward a lasting, holistic solution known as LIFT Orlando, which has the tagline "Breaking the cycle of poverty through neighborhood revitalization."

Their goal is transformation, not a patch or a platitude. As Hogan said, "It comes down to Jesus' statement, 'Do unto others as you would have them do unto you.' And, 'To those to whom much is given, much is required.'" LIFT Orlando is one of the many examples of igniting the power of business to make our communities better, which is what a healthy balance of the natural and the spiritual are all about. But it doesn't begin in a project or an organization; it begins in our hearts.

People want to work with a person, not for a company. Most (of our people) feel that this is more than just a job. They feel either a divine calling or the satisfaction of a desire to make a difference in the world.
—S. Trewitt Cathy, Chick-fil-A

••••••• DOG BONES: •••••••

1. **Faith gives** us the confidence to venture and to believe we aren't alone in our initiatives. That there is one who loves us and is committed to our well-being, who celebrates and motivates our endeavors, who is both mentor and backer. That inspiration and ideas have a source; therefore, are worth the risk and the sacrifice it takes to achieve them. That even when we fail, we aren't failures; rather, there are lessons to learn, and we simply need to learn the lesson, get up, and start again. Do you have that kind of faith operating in your life?

2. **Faith provides** significance that isn't based on aptitude, appearance, or accomplishments. We all are searching for significance. As Mr. Banks sang in *Mary Poppins*, "A man has dreams of walking with giants, to carve his niche on the edifice of time." That is something we all want and need. But what happens if we fall short like Mr. Banks did? Who hasn't failed and questioned their life's meaning? Equally perplexing, how do you explain the people who are wildly successful, who achieve fame and fortune, only to find they are still empty and the prize has left them unsatisfied? We were made to achieve, but we need something beyond it to anchor our lives. Much of what we think is significant is a cultural construct that can change as quickly as hairstyles or car models; one doctor visit, one serious accident, one change in the market can cause it all to crash. Do you have the kind of faith that can give significance to the homeless individual trying to find a job or the executive struggling with alcoholism?

3. **Faith motivates** us to look at ourselves and others differently. We have known atheists who have a high regard for people and want to make life better, perhaps because they believe this is all the life there ever will be. However, faith admonishes us to view others and ourselves with a sense of value and esteem, because we are endowed with worth by our Creator. Christians are, in fact, commanded to value others and see people as a masterpiece forged by the ultimate designer. Our faith isn't just about where we are going to go, but the meaning behind why Jesus came and the difference we are to make here, in light of that. Are you able to view even people who are your enemies, by choice

or by circumstance, with the same esteem and respect as your closest relative?

4. **Faith causes accountability** to certain guidelines that, like the values of an organization, should be the criteria we use to make decisions every day. Someone once said, "Honesty isn't the best policy, it is the only policy." Questions like: Should I steal? Should I treat this person in a demeaning way? Should I nurture hatred or resentment? Should I make an unseemly sexual comment to a co-worker? These are questions we don't have to ask because the answer has already been provided by our faith. Like our republic, where the Constitution is seen as higher than any politician, judge, CEO, general, or journalist, so values rooted in something higher than ourselves keep us in balance and help us avoid many of the moral entanglements that can derail our lives. Do you have a faith that provides these absolutes?

CHAPTER 10

Being the Person Your Dog Thinks You Are
Building a Legacy

If you would not be forgotten as soon as you are dead, either write something worth reading or do something worth being written about.
—Benjamin Franklin

There is a growing fascination with history in our culture. This is partly because educators began to de-emphasize the subject in favor of "social studies" in the late 1960s, so many Baby Boomers grew up largely ignorant of their historic roots. Also, history has been the target of not only massive reinterpretation, but pure invention to support certain cultural or political agendas. So, thoughtful individuals have delved into the historic records to mine and mint fresh accounts of our predecessors' stories.

History holds a unique power. President Harry Truman said, "The only thing new in the world is the history you don't know." Every time we turn on a light, press a remote control, or study market research, we are predicting what could happen next, based on what did happen in the past. This is the power of history—it forecasts or at least shapes our view of what the future holds.

British novelist George Orwell put it this way: "Whoever controls the past, controls the future." In other words, whoever is interpreting the past shapes our expectations of what tomorrow will bring. For instance, historians agree the lack of resolve on the part of Western democracies was a key factor in allowing the rise of Hitler's Third Reich. So, a different approach was taken to the aggression of the Soviet Union, which resulted in a different outcome. Orwell went on to say, "Whoever controls the present, controls the past," or history is written by the ones in power in the present. So, yesterday's heroes can become today's villains, depending on how the story is being told.

This is what a legacy is all about; it is a past helping shape a preferred future. It is the collective story of our family, our nation, or our business and the impact it can have on others. It is the social, spiritual, psychological, and even entrepreneurial DNA that is passed down to us and from us to others.

Sometimes that legacy is the influence of a parent, teacher, coach, or mentor; sometimes it is the impact of an innovation or discovery changing the course of nations. Like the novels of James Michener or Edward Rutherford, legacy is our part in the flow of history and something we all want to shape.

Faster Than You Think

Perhaps shaping a legacy isn't as complicated as one might think. If our culture were to embrace the legacy of the entrepreneurs who have gone before us and now surround us, transforming America and the rest of the world into an entrepreneurial-driven and culture-influencing movement could render outcomes beyond our dreams.

We don't think legacy can or should be left to chance. We make our legacy with the decisions we make every day. As the old maxim puts it, "Sow a thought, and you reap an action; sow an act, and you reap a habit; sow a habit, and you reap a character; sow a character, and you reap a destiny." Our intentionality and design accelerates everything.

For instance, how long did it take for a wolf to become man's best friend and companion, the dog? We all know domesticated dogs are the descendants of wolves. But wolves, like other wild members of the canine family, can't be tamed. Though they seem like other dogs when they are pups, as they mature the wild side kicks in and, aside from extremely rare instances, any kind of real domestication isn't successful.

Dmitri K. Belyaev, a Russian scientist, may have done more than anyone to explain the process by which wolves were transformed into our four-legged buddies. The dog/man partnership may have started as early as twelve thousand years ago and perhaps much earlier. His research demonstrates not only how, but the accelerated pace in which it could have happened. Belyaev's study didn't focus on dogs or wolves, but on foxes; however, his research provides very credible evidence on how predators become pets.

Much of Belyaev's research was done clandestinely because the communists initially branded genetics as "fascist science" because of the way the Nazis were manipulating it for their "super race" propaganda. What his team did was, starting with silver fox pups at one month old and continuing to sexual maturity at seven to eight months, they rated the fox's response when approached by and fed by humans. It was a tameness test. Would the fox try to bite the experimenters if they attempted to touch it? The more affable foxes were separated, and about 20 percent of those most willing to interact positively with humans were bred.

In just 40 generations, he produced a breed of friendly, domesticated foxes. They liked hanging out with humans, did displays to attract favorable attention, and licked their caretaker's hands. In the process, researchers noticed physical changes in fur coloration, even in the shape of their skulls, jaws, and teeth—plus they lost the "musky fox smell."

It demonstrates how quickly characteristics leading to a certain outcome can be inculcated when they are recognized, reinforced, rewarded, and replicated.

Never Losing His Edge

"There are certain things that are fundamental to human fulfillment," the late author and leadership educator Dr. Stephen Covey once said. "The essence of these needs is captured in the phrase, 'to live, to love, to learn, to leave a legacy.'" After elaborating on the others, he concluded, "The need to leave a legacy is our spiritual need to have a sense of meaning, purpose, personal congruence, and contribution."

We couldn't agree with Covey more. Legacy is one of our primal drives. What it means and how it is expressed differs from person to person, but its significance doesn't vary.

Jeff Piersall recalls clearly when this principle really dawned on him: "I was sitting in a seminar room that was large enough to hold fifteen-hundred people, and there was not an empty seat in the place. It was understandable—the crowd at the Direct Selling Association (DSA) convention was about to hear from one of the Babe Ruths in the pantheon of not just the DSA, but business itself.

"He stood for everything that was right and purposeful about being an entrepreneur; yet as usual, there were those who didn't grasp his place in the history of the free enterprise system. Richard 'Rich' DeVos, the co-founder and rainmaker for Amway Corporation whose family owns the Orlando Magic, was about to take the stage.

"Amway is the single largest brand in the direct sales industry, producing more than $8 billion in worldwide sales annually. At the time, I was CEO of an up-and-coming direct sales company that had grown, in three-and-a-half years, from a half-million in sales to $35 million annually. Honestly, I wasn't expecting much. I had met Rich DeVos, who was then almost 80, and assumed he was out of touch with the industry, but I was about to be humbled.

"After being introduced by his son Dick, DeVos simply told his story, commenting, 'I have told my story for fifty years.' Then he added, 'Can you tell your story? The number one fundamental in business is, tell your story!'

"One would think DeVos' story would be all about the industry, but it was all about life, because to DeVos that is what business is—life. *If there is only one thing you take from this book*, it would be what I learned from his presentation that day, and I made sure it became part of my life philosophy: his explanation of the four stages of life; and now I hope it will become a part of your philosophy."

Our personal ventures, our relationships, organizations, churches, schools, communities, and governments all go through each of these stages. No one is immune to any stage. The secret is understanding and identifying where you are in the continuum so you can take corrective measures.

1. The first stage of life he explained is the **BUILD/CREATE** stage. This is where we all want to be because it is full of excitement and joy. This is where you make things happen; in fact, we are convinced you are intended by your Creator to not visit but to live in this stage. This is why starting a business is so exciting and why we determine to work through the challenges. It is in the essence of our DNA.

2. The second is the **MANAGEMENT** stage. As passion starts to wane, it is easy to fall for the misconception that you can manage others to do the building and creating for you. This isn't delegating; it is abdicating your primary and primal responsibility. In so doing, you put your relationship or business on autopilot and move from growth to maintenance. You move into a protective or a defensive posture versus a positive offensive posture. Inevitably, if you do not pull yourself out of the Management stage, you will fall into stage three.

   Talking to one of our close friends Bernie Simpkins, a successful entrepreneur and philanthropist, as he went into retirement from the oil distribution business, he made an insightful comment. "It is so much easier to build wealth than preserve it because building is positive and the act of preservation is all about avoiding risk; it's managing the negative."

3. Stage Three is the **DEFENDER OF NO GROWTH** stage. In this stage, you find and reiterate all the good reasons why your business or your relationships are no longer building, creating, or growing. The economy is bad, the market changed, capital tightened, people just don't want to work…and on, and on, and on. Jeff says his company, SCB Marketing, was started in 2006 and never even knew there was a recession until it was already over. If you stay in the Defender of No Growth stage, you will eventually slip into the final fatal stage.

4. Stage Four is the **BLAME** stage. Here you start shifting responsibility. Responsibility is the power to make a response or a decision that can change outcomes you control. When we blame others, we empower them instead of ourselves, and the only person whose actions and decisions we can really control are our own. Essentially, we are making a mental and emotional exit to justify the actual exit, which is rapidly approaching.

What happens in relationships when the excuses turn into blame? Divorce! Much of our frustration with government is that it is constantly looking for scapegoats instead of solutions.

"These are the four principles Rich DeVos shared with me (I felt like I was the only person in the room at the time) and I use them to evaluate where I am every day," Jeff said. "It is the legacy left to one young upstart that I will never forget."

From the Ground Up

When you understand legacy, you see how it shapes us, our institutions, and our expectations. How many cultures are defined by an aspiration like "The American Dream?" It is a goal that has and, in all likelihood, always will cause us to be a people on the move. Early settlers pushed steadily westward, and every transportation breakthrough from the steamboat to the locomotive to eventually the car and the plane became means of chasing that elusive hope defining us as a people. This quest for new opportunity in new places is in every American's personal and cultural DNA, perhaps because all of us are either immigrants or their descendants.

One of the unfortunate consequences of our questing culture is, unless you subscribe to Ancestry.com, in all likelihood you know very little about your great-grandparents. Most Americans don't even know their names or anything of significance about their stories. There are a few rare families that are able to reach and expand while maintaining an uncanny sense of not only heritage but the values that guided their forebearer. As mentioned before, one of our personal heroes of legacy is Joseph Duda. The company he served as CEO, A. Duda and Sons, is now in the fifth generation of family ownership and continues to grow in size and influence.

Joseph's grandfather, Andrew, came from Slovakia, which before World War I was a part of the Austro-Hungarian empire. Change in most of Eastern Europe, particularly social change, came much slower than it did in the West. But Andrew Duda was a young man with vision and determination that was deeply rooted in his Lutheran faith. So much so that nearly one hundred years later, his grandson Joseph would call one of the largest and most successful planned communities in Florida and home to nearly fifteen-thousand people, "Viera," as an acknowledgment of his forebearer's convictions. "Viera" is Slovak for "faith."

Though he probably pondered and planned for years, in 1909, Andrew Duda decided to act on his dream. Living like his forefathers before him on land that was controlled by the aristocracy was not what he wanted for himself or his sons. He knew the only place he could go where land ownership could be a reality was America. Therefore, in a move that may seem audacious to many today, he embarked alone to establish a life where his wife, daughter, and three young sons could later join him.

Three years later, he was leaving the general store in Oviedo, Florida, now on the eastern outskirts of Orlando, and as he walked along the dirt road, a horse-drawn carriage arrived in town with his family on board. He was totally unprepared for their arrival, even though his wife had sent a telegram three weeks earlier. The telegram arrived on the same carriage as his family.

He moved his family into a literal shack, where workers for an abandoned turpentine distillery had lived. Joseph's father once told him, "The place was easy to clean; you could sweep the dirt right through the cracks in the floor." It was a valiant effort, but he soon realized he was losing ground. So, he moved his young family back to Cleveland, where he had worked in a furniture factory, and got his family out of the city to a rural home, where his sons could make extra money raising vegetables while avoiding the influences of a growing industrial city.

Twelve years later, Andrew was ready to launch out again and return to the land he had bought in Central Florida. This time he had a young and willing workforce, his three sons. Rather than going their separate ways; John, Andrew Jr., and Ferdinand decided their best chance of success would come by sticking together. This was a decision that carried them and their heirs from 40 acres of celery in Oviedo to agricultural and real estate holdings that include tens of thousands of acres in Florida, along with substantial holdings in Georgia, Texas, California, and twelve other states, generating more than $440 million a year in revenue and producing almost 33 percent of the celery consumed in the U.S.

Stewards of the Land

Joseph was a third-generation Duda, growing up in the business and near his grandfather, who for the last 20 years of his life lived in their home. Andrew Sr. however, wasn't very talkative, as Slovak was his first language and English was a language of necessity only. "He would be sitting on the porch when I got home from school, and we wouldn't say much. Now, I look back and think of all the things I could have learned from him."

However, that wasn't something Joseph's father did. "I never had a doubt I would work for the family business. I suppose part of that was because early on my father and my uncles regularly talked with my brothers and cousins about the company. They shared their mistakes and their successes, along with the desire to leave the business to the family, to build a legacy." Few young people today are privy to that kind of inspiration and insight.

The lessons weren't just learned during those informal training sessions; it was a lifestyle of mentorship. "My father wanted us to learn the value of work, so I started on the farm when I was twelve. Well… what does a twelve-year-old kid do?" Then, chuckling in his distinctive

Southern drawl, he answered, "Get in the way. Actually, my father told my foreman that if I didn't work to send me home.

"I knew then farming wasn't for me, but in a couple of years, I went to work on the ranch," which still exists near the community of Viera, occupying almost fifteen-thousand acres in Brevard County, near the home of Kennedy Space Center and Cape Canaveral. "I said to myself, 'This is where I want to be—horses, cows, wide-open spaces,' in fact, that is what I planned to do for the rest of my life. I didn't even want to go to college; I wanted to go to work right out of high school. But I had some solid mentors who advised me to add formal education to my experience, which I did at the University of Florida."

Although they are highly successful in ranching and agriculture, the Dudas have a faith paradigm that causes them to see themselves as "stewards of the land." As Joseph rose in authority in the family enterprise, he saw that perhaps a better use for a portion of the ranch would be as a master planned community, and today almost half of the property is a nature preserve along the St. Johns River. In those early years, his bond, not only to the Duda ranch but to the area, began to take root.

"I always felt this county was perfect," he said. "It isn't in the mainstream of Orlando, but if you want that, you can go over there for a few days and enjoy the theme parks or the city, then you can come back here to live."

He freely admits, "I'm a vision guy; I would rather spend my time thinking about what and where we ought to be rather than what and where we are. Most people have a 'show me' perspective on life. There aren't that many of us (visionaries), and admittedly I tend to get ahead of people, sometimes way too far. Then, I have to come back and show folks how to catch up. In fact, I come from a family that's very pragmatic, very 'show me' oriented, at least most of them, and I have found myself at odds because I get way ahead of them in my thinking."

He continued, "It is vision that unites and motivates people to a common and achievable goal. I love the visioning processes of challenging our mindsets and challenging the status quo, imagining what you could be, thinking about tomorrow and losing your fixation on yesterday. Our uncles were incredible in allowing us and supporting us in building our dreams. All my brothers and cousins had aspirations; some of our plans were successful, some weren't, but overall more were successful than not. I admit one or two of my ideas out of five might not be so great, but three of them could really work! That was their approach—you learn by trying, and it's always been my approach as well."

That is our real legacy: not really the business we build, because that could be sold; not the building we construct, because that could be repurposed. Legacy is the impact we make on people, the part of us that is planted and grows in others, the human canvas on which we paint the true masterpieces.

Today, Viera continues its infill, a plan that will go on for the next twenty-plus years. It is the home to thousands of residents; the most celebrated restaurants and shopping venues in the area; hospitals and schools; the seat of the county's government, justice, and school system; and, a stadium that has served as the spring training home of the Florida Marlins and the Washington Nationals. But something else captures Joseph's heart: "This community is where families are making their memories, building their legacies. When I drive through Viera and see all the churches that dot the community, I think, 'Maybe that is the reason we developed this community. To give all these people the opportunity to experience the faith heritage I was raised in, and that has shaped my life.'"

Success without a successor is failure.
—Myles Munroe

• • • • • • • DOG BONES: • • • • • • •

1. **Legacy is where your vision lives on beyond you.** Many of the most noble and influential visions are never realized by the vision's originator. Often, the visionary pioneer simply blazes the trail where others one day will build an interstate highway. How much did those two brothers see when they successfully tested their aircraft in Kitty Hawk, North Carolina, back in 1903?

2. **Success is something you attract** by becoming the person you want others to be. Stop trying to change everyone else and start working on you. If you can become the individual you would like everyone else to be, the world will be a better place; it is called personal accountability. Remember what author Jeff Olsen said, "If you are on the success curve you are pulled by the future; people on the failure curve are pulled by the past."

3. **Success is that place in the road** where opportunity and preparation intersect, missed by so many because it comes disguised as hard work. As Lincoln said, "I get ready, and perhaps my chance will come." Once you are prepared, then opportunity presents itself, but not if you are afraid because of the long hours, the possible failure, and mostly the dogged hard work it will take to become successful.

4. **Our legacy rests on one foundation.** The influence we have and how we are remembered often has more to do with our character than it does our accomplishments. When Harris Rosen, the highly successful Central Florida hotelier and philanthropist, was asked to come to his alma mater, Cornell University, and lecture on ethics, he declined the

offer. His response, "Why give a lecture on ethics? It is easy; just do the right thing."

CONCLUSION

We're Not in Kansas, Toto
Courage

*Courage is rightly esteemed the first of human qualities
because it is the quality which guarantees all others.*
—Winston Churchill

We have provided you with ten proven virtues to build a successful business:

1. **The Foundation of Trust**
2. **Relational Priority**
3. **Diversity of Expression**
4. **Influence, Not Imposition**
5. **The Significance of Synergy**
6. **Prevailing Vision**
7. **Process Orientation**
8. **Validating Desire**
9. **Life is Both Natural and Spiritual**
10. **Building a Legacy**

Yet, none of these can be achieved without the one virtue that is the sum total of all virtues—**COURAGE.**

For generations, L. Frank Baum's classic story *The Wizard of Oz* has been etched into our collective childhood memory. Now the famous line, "Toto, I have a feeling we're not in Kansas, anymore," has passed into popular vernacular to describe the wonder of encountering a new and unfamiliar place or opportunity. Each of the central characters in the story represents a quest we all are on and a discovery it is essential for each of us to make.

Dorothy comes to the realization that what she longs for is not a fantasy adventure in some exotic place, but the relationships that define her home. Like many things about this allegorical saga, the fact that the story centered on a heroine who gradually realized her untapped leadership potential, and that even the villain was a woman, showed the farsighted respect Baum had for what was then considered "the fairer sex."

You laugh, or maybe you're taken aback, but Dorothy is the one who inspired and encouraged her three fellow travelers to believe there was something in them that others couldn't see and to join her on the dream quest. Plus, she not only faced down the Wicked Witch of the West, but it was Dorothy, along with her faithful companion Toto, who pulled back the curtain to expose Oz's leading citizen and put him in his place.

Dorothy's companions give us an important insight into what tends to hold us back. It was Dorothy's faith, persistence, and willingness to lead, even though Oz was way outside her comfort zone, that brought hope and realization to everyone. As Ginni Rometty, who is chair, president, and CEO of IBM, once said: "I learned to always take on things I'd never done before. Growth and comfort do not coexist."

If I Only Had a...

For Dorothy, the brainless scarecrow was closest to her heart and is certainly the quality most of us think we lack in pursuing our dreams. Remember what he said when he got his Th.D., "Doctor of Thinkology?" "The sum of the square roots of any two sides of an isosceles triangle is equal to the square root of the remaining side. Oh joy! Rapture! I've got a brain!" Of course, he didn't exactly get the Pythagorean Theorem correct but how many actually knew that?

Sara Blakely, who by her mid-40s had amassed a fortune of approximately $1 billion thanks to her Spanx line of undergarments and now jeans and yoga wear, said: "Don't be intimidated by what you don't know. That can be your greatest strength and ensure that you do things differently from everyone else."

The Tin Woodman was searching for the second life essential, a heart. When push comes to shove, in every endeavor in life, the Tinman was right; it is passion that carries the day. As Beethoven said, "To play a wrong note is insignificant; to play without passion is inexcusable." The reason so much ink has been spilt on the subject of *attitude* is because it serves as both the gas that ignites our entrepreneurial engine and the oil that keeps friction from burning up our relationships. If you aren't sure about the power of passion and heart, watch the films *Rudy* or *Eddie the Eagle*, and ask yourself why you found them so inspiring. Science is uncovering how our mindsets literally align our neuropathways, which shape how we perceive and interpret reality, either positively or negatively.

However, brains and passion, as crucial as they are, have to be engaged. They must be turned into action, and only one thing can do that: courage. It was the Cowardly Lion who completed the triad and was actually at the center of all the others' qualities.

Eleanor Roosevelt must have identified with this timid "King of the Forest," because she once said, "Do one thing every day that scares you," and then added, "You gain strength and confidence by every experience in which you really stop to look fear in the face. You are able to say to yourself, 'I lived through this horror. I can take the next thing that comes along.' You must do the thing you think you cannot do."

> In the Cowardly Lion's own words:
> *What makes a king out of a slave? Courage!*
> *What makes the flag on the mast to wave? Courage!*
> *What makes the elephant charge his tusk in the misty mist, or the dusky dusk? Courage!*
> *What makes the muskrat guard his musk? Courage!*
> *What makes the Hottentot so hot?*
> *What puts the "ape" in apricot?*
> *What have they got that I ain't got?*
> Dorothy, Scarecrow and the Tin Woodman reply: *Courage!*
> Cowardly Lion: *You can say that again!*

C.S. Lewis, author of *The Chronicles of Narnia* as well as a host of philosophical and theological works, made the same point. "Courage", he wrote, "is not simply one of the virtues, but the form of **every virtue** at the testing point."

In other words, every quality or value that we esteem is simply a lofty sentiment or an elusive ideal unless activated by courage. What good is hope, if at that crucial moment when hope is required we cave into despair? Or what is the benefit of honesty, if we find it is safer and more convenient to shade the truth when the heat is on? Courage is that compass which focuses us away from our feelings or circumstances and on those things that are higher than ourselves. This is why in every culture and throughout history, it is one of the qualities we celebrate.

Most of us are well-intentioned, but the tires that give traction to our intentions are usually daring acts. What carries intentions that begin nobly to a meaningful and lasting conclusion? It is undoubtedly the courage to persevere through the inevitable obstacles and setbacks that always stand between a vision's conception and its realization. The majority of organizations like churches are formed around noble intentions, but they don't always produce outstanding results. One observer commented, "Most churches aren't built with bad people. They are primarily composed of good people, but who are afraid to do anything—they are good…for nothing." Ouch!

There aren't any courses on courage that we know of, nor is there a group you can join that will convey courage upon you, like Toastmasters can help with public speaking. We have observed, however, that if you associate with courageous people, their courage will infect you. In fact, the word *encouragement* means to put or add courage to someone. On the other hand, *discouragement* comes from being with anxious people who fill you with apprehension, excessive caution, and ultimately paralysis.

Of course, the presence of fear is not what makes one a coward. Mountain climbers and battle-hardened soldiers all have fear. It is how they manage and direct that fear that makes them so admirable. Few people choose the circumstances that reveal their courage. Heroes aren't born; in most cases, they are cornered. As the great U.S. naval officer Admiral William "Bull" Halsey said, "There are no great men, there are only ordinary men who because of extraordinary circumstances are forced to meet great challenges." Most of us, like the Cowardly Lion, find reservoirs of courage we didn't know existed when faced with situations that are beyond us. Courage, like a mechanic selecting the proper tool, acts as the catalyst empowering us to choose the right virtue at the right time.

No Guts, No Glory

Have you heard of Larry Walters, or at least of his stunt? It certainly would have qualified for a Darwin Award, had he not been miraculously rescued. Darwin Awards are tongue-in-cheek honors that recognize individuals whose actions are so ill-thought-out that they contribute to human evolution by selecting themselves out of the gene pool by death or sterilization.

It seems Larry always wanted to be a pilot but was prevented from qualifying for the Air Force's flight school because of his poor eyesight. Instead, he became an aircraft mechanic. After retirement, still longing to soar, he bought a tank of helium and 45 surplus weather balloons. He strapped the balloons to a lawn chair and intended to use a pellet gun to control his altitude and ascent by puncturing the balloons. When the intrepid balloonist cut his anchor ropes, instead of making a slow ascent he shot like a rocket up to eleven-thousand feet. Fortunately, he was saved from colliding with a 747 aircraft by a Coast Guard helicopter. When asked why he had attempted this feat, he said, "You can't just sit around all your life."

Though one might wonder who would let a guy like Larry tinker around on a jet aircraft, we all admire those who are willing to take the risks that inevitably lead to great success. As Theodore Roosevelt said, "It is impossible to win the great prizes of life without running risks." Or Italian poet and opera librettist Pietro Metastasio who said, "Every noble acquisition is attended with its risks; he who fears to encounter the one must not expect to attain the other."

When Jim Burke became the head of a new products division at Johnson & Johnson, one of his first projects was the development of a children's chest rub. Unfortunately, the product failed miserably. When he was called in to see the CEO, Burke expected to be fired. However, he was met with a surprising reception. "Are you the one who just cost us all that money?" asked Robert Wood Johnson. Burke, of course, nodded. "Well, I just want to congratulate you. If you are making mistakes, that means you are taking risks, and we won't grow unless you take risks!"

Some years later, when Burke himself became CEO of Johnson & Johnson, he continued to spread that word.

What makes most of us so averse to risk is simply a fear of failure, or more precisely, how we view our failures. Thomas Edison said, "There is only one good idea in one-hundred, so I want to discover the ninety-nine failures as quickly as possible."

Craig McCaw was a pioneer in the cellular phone business, but few of us have ever heard of him. In his biography, *Money From Thin Air*, he tells how he started McCaw Cellular Communications in 1976, just three years out of college. Eighteen years later, he sold his company to AT&T for $16.5 billion. Not too shabby for a fellow who is dyslexic and got C's and D's in college.

One of his competitors, Jack Roberts, said of him, "Craig's strength is bold risks. His thinking is visionary, and he is willing to play close to the edge." H. Hershel Shosteck of *Forbes* magazine wrote: "Mr. McCaw hired people he trusted and gave them lots of room to get results. He gave a lot of autonomy to his subordinates, and they took the ball and ran with it."

McCaw himself said, "The greatest burden you can ever put on someone is trust," which is the consummate relational risk. In fact, trust in ourselves, our experience, our foresight, or others is the flip side of the same coin we call risk.

Though the Craig McCaws of the world are celebrated for their risk tolerance, it's important to realize his risks were mediated by an understanding of where the market was heading and how to position himself to capitalize on it. As George Patton said, "Take calculated risks. That is quite different from being rash." Nevertheless, taking those risks is crucial. As one writer said, "Progress means taking risks, for you can't steal home and keep your foot on third base."

138 | Dogs Don't Bark at Parked Cars™

A Resilient Life

Courage is about our direction in life and determination to get there, come what may. Any vision we pursue is like what aeronautical engineers discovered when they were trying to break the sound barrier. Essentially, as planes got closer to the speed of sound, sound waves built up on the front of the aircraft wings, sometimes shredding them to pieces. When Chuck Yeager broke the sound barrier on October 14, 1947, in Bell X-1, the sound waves shifted from in front of the wing to behind it, producing the characteristic "sonic boom."

For the entrepreneur, a similar resistance always builds up in front of our efforts, and it is most intense right before we break through it. However, it isn't always going faster; many times, it is plodding forward a few miles per hour like Columbus did in the Santa Maria. We call this resilience, and it begins with knowing where we are headed. Otherwise, we are like Alice in Wonderland and the insightful conversation she had with the ever-smiling Cheshire Cat.

Coming to a fork in the road, Alice asks: *"Would you please tell me which way I ought to go from here?"*
The cat responds: *"That depends a great deal on where you want to get to."*
Alice answers: *"I don't much care where —"*
Then the cat says: *"Then it doesn't matter which way you go."*
To clarify Alice says: *"So long as I get SOMEWHERE."*
The cat grins: *"Oh, you are sure to do that...if only you walk long enough."*

Everyone gets "somewhere" in life; the difference-makers determine where they want to go and what it will take to get there. Otherwise, we're like Lily Tomlin, who once said, "I always wanted to be somebody, but now I realize I should have been more specific."

Writer Gordon MacDonald in his book *A Resilient Life* quotes Thomas Merton to identify the two questions we need to ask about our primary purpose in life.

"If you want to identify me, ask me not where I live or what I like to eat or how I comb my hair. Instead, ask me what I think I am living for, in detail, and ask me what I think is keeping me from living fully the thing I want to live for. Between these two answers, you can determine the identity of any person. The better answer he has, the more of a person he is."

As challenging as it may be to ask ourselves these questions, what may prove even more challenging is staying on course once we decide where we want to go. Like the cow staring over the fence at the patch of green that is just out of reach, the lure of the instant is almost irresistible. However, it is those who stay on target, who delay their gratification, who see life as a marathon, not as a sprint, who truly finish well.

See You at the Finish

Stephen Ambrose is one of our favorite history writers. Books like *Undaunted Courage* about Lewis and Clark and the celebrated *Band of Brothers* are a few of his works. He is at his best in *Nothing Like it in the World*, which chronicles the building of the transcontinental railroad. According to Ambrose, it was not only an unrivaled engineering feat, it was the primary building block of our expanding nation linking America from sea to shining sea.

One of the opening scenes of the book was when construction began on the western leg, building from California eastward. A huge celebration to commemorate "driving the first spike" was planned. Collis Huntington, one of those who became known as "The Big 4" financial backers, was of course invited, but he declined to attend.

He wrote the organizers, "If you want to celebrate the driving of the first spike, go ahead and do it. I don't. Those mountains over there look too ugly. We may fail, and if we do, I want to have as few people to know it as we can." Adding, "Anybody can drive the first spike, but there are months of labor and unrest between the first and the last spike."

Isn't it interesting how many runners are lined up to start the Boston Marathon? The finish is always less congested and usually single file. Or how each year we celebrate our birthday, which though significant, we had absolutely nothing to do with. In life, it is the path we choose to take and our resilience to finish that determines our destiny. Like the telegraph sent to President Ulysses S. Grant in May of 1869, "Sir, we have the honor to report that the last rail is laid, the last spike is driven, the Pacific Railroad is finished." This is the true reward.

Pay Day, Some Day

The quality of courage is present in every successful entrepreneur on the planet and often even in many of the unsuccessful ones. We could almost say "entrepreneur" and "courage" are somewhat synonymous, though the entrepreneur himself rarely is perceived in those terms.

Much like the stories that have come out of Silicon Valley, Central Florida has a growing cadre of entrepreneurs focusing on a new technology. Gutenberg's printing press, Watt's steam engine, Wright's airplane, Kilby and Noyce's silicon chip, Steve Wozniak's personal computer, are all recognized as disruptive technologies, changing the course of history and the way modern man lives. But what if a technology emerged that changed the way people learned? Wouldn't that be as disruptive as the development of the alphabet?

That "what if" is a reality, and Central Florida has emerged as the epicenter of this transformative technology known as "modeling and simulation." One of our favorite entrepreneurs, Waymon Armstrong, president and CEO of Engineering & Computer Simulations Inc.

(ECS), is one of this sector's success stories. To him "the possibilities are limitless" when it comes to modeling, simulation, and training.

Instead of using two-dimensional architectural renderings or bulky models to help clients get a visual understanding of a building, now they can take a virtual tour, walk right into the building's lobby, or enjoy a panoramic view from the 30th floor. Simulations have moved beyond only training pilots, to equipping combat medics to respond to wounded soldiers or preparing emergency response teams for disaster events, and even how to perform complex surgical procedures. And that is the tip of the iceberg; it is the undiscovered country of revolutionizing the way we learn and using visualization to refine the decision-making process.

As cutting-edge as simulation is, building a business that can catch and ride that wave of innovation is no easy task. Armstrong said, smiling, "A book I'm working through suggested that the odds are so stacked against you, entrepreneurs should be recognized and awarded by the government just below returning veterans. If you get wounded in battle, you get a Purple Heart; there should be something like that for entrepreneurs who come back after inevitable failures."

He added, "Entrepreneurship is messy; it's hard work; it's all about delayed gratification. Moreover, it isn't only the entrepreneurs who need the inspiration; it is the people who work with them and their families."

The journey for Armstrong began when he saw the power of simulation at what is now Martin Marietta in Orlando. The company he was with at the time didn't share his commitment to the technology, so he decided to branch out on his own and, in May of 1997, he started ECS. He realized then in the government sector what he sees now in the commercial sector. "No one has made simulation ubiquitous or pervasive. It is utilized in various industries, but the fields are ripe in countless other arenas," he beamed.

However, by 2001, ECS was struggling to stay afloat. The dot-com industry had become the dot-bomb, and life-giving capital was being stretched thinner and thinner. Employees stayed on without pay while Armstrong racked up about $700,000 in credit card debt, back payroll, and lease exposure.

"I'm turning 40, my wife and I had our first child, and the one glimmer of hope was that all the debt was in my name—my wife's credit was pristine. So, I went to her, explained the situation, and she not only went back to work to support us, she borrowed to keep us afloat."

Today, Armstrong's wife Frances serves as CEO. "We had to work together," Frances reflected. "I held two jobs and came in the office on the weekends to work with Waymon, assisting where I could." Armstrong had to obtain legal protection, not to erase his debts, but to buy time until he could pay them. Since 2004, ECS has been on a steady growth trend, and he added proudly, "By 2009, we had paid everyone off in full." Paying off his debts was a position that surprised his legal advisers and bolstered his reputation.

Living on vision, drive, and a string of credit cards, Armstrong hit trade shows and knocked on every door of opportunity, evangelizing for the technology and his company. Armstrong's string of success has been without remission and has inspired a host of growing simulation startups in the region.

Interestingly, it is the Department of Defense that has led the way in digital education, which is not surprising because the DoD trains more employees in mission-critical tasks than any organization in the world. The results have been astounding. The number of fatalities in the "platinum hour" (the first hour after being wounded) was 24 percent in the Vietnam War. Thanks to dramatic improvements in body armor, along with combat wound treatment and care using simulation training, that number dropped to six percent in the Middle East conflict.

A doctoral candidate conducted a study on 300 Army and Marine personnel to compare knowledge retention using different training methods. The research compared hearing a lecture and seeing a PowerPoint versus seeing a PowerPoint and playing a game simulation. The Army participants showed a nine percent spike in retention and the Marines eleven percent when using simulation.

That is the power of "what if." To Armstrong and other innovators in the modeling and simulation industry, it is the future. In addition, it plays to the sweet spot of people in the next generation. Armstrong describes them as "digital natives" and says he still considers himself a "digital immigrant."

The essence of the entrepreneur or starter is the ability not only to see a future trend but to have the courage; and therefore, make the sacrifice to make that trend a reality. It requires the kind of leadership audacity seen in Hernando Cortez when he arrived in Mexico in 1519. In order to prevent a mutiny and to focus his small contingency on the prize before them, in what is today Mexico City, he scuttled or burned his own ships. When his men asked how they would get home, he replied, "If we are going home, we are going home in their ships!"

The catalyst for everything is the courage to ignore the barking dogs and to set your face like a flint on the prize set before you.

Better to try and fail, than fail to try.
—Winston Churchill

1. **You will pay a price in life.** The price every human pays is either regret or discipline. Regret for the things we didn't do, which we should have done, or the discipline to delay

gratification and pay the price in the present for what is desired in the future. Regret over the things we did and yet failed, or were errors in judgment, may be tempered with time. Regret for the things we did not do—that's inconsolable.

2. **Remember the definition of faith and fear.** They are exactly the same—"our perspective on the unseen things in our future." How you choose to view your future creates a dramatic difference. Faith doesn't remove fear; faith is the strength to act in spite of fear.

3. **Courage is expressed in persistence.** Once, Churchill was asked to speak during the war at his alma mater. After the lengthy introduction, he went to the podium and said, "Never give up!" Then sat down. The people on the stage began to look confused, and the crowd began to murmur. So, seeing the reaction, he returned to the podium and said, "Never, never, never give up!" And again, sat down. Jesus said, "Ask, and it will be given unto you. Seek, and you will find. Knock, and the door will be open."

Your daily prayer: God Grant me the serenity to accept the people I cannot change, the courage to change the one I can, and the wisdom to know it's me.

"KEEP MOVING"

by Wes Piersall, son of author Jeff Piersall

Life is a journey that will take you many places
And along the way, you'll meet many new faces
The world around us will continuously change
And for many, this idea could seem strange

There will be mountains to climb and not always sunshine
And along the way there will be some holding stop signs
Becoming successful will not happen overnight
And people around you won't always think it's right

So, keep the right people close to your side
And when you get challenged never run or hide
On the path to greatness you reach beyond comfort zones
But just remember where you came from and you're never alone

You can't be like the Cowardly Lion
Because a lack of courage keeps one from tryin'
Courage is not something that can be bought at the store
And you won't find it by aimlessly going door to door

It's the internal flame that burns within us all
When we use it, we are able to move forward and not stall
Always stay hungry, never be satisfied
Remember the times you failed, the times you cried

Not everyone will agree with what you're trying to do
But that's okay because all you need is YOU!
Learn when to work and learn when to play
Know when to love and when you need to pray

Always be courageous and shoot for the stars
And remember, dogs don't bark at parked cars!!!

JEFF PIERSALL BIO

Jeff Piersall is a proven leader in all endeavors of his life having positively affected thousands of people throughout his career. He possesses the unique ability to abridge current circumstances with future foresights.

As Founder and CEO of SCB Marketing, Jeff inspires, motivates and connects entrepreneurs, business leaders and communities through his four business journals, numerous specialty publications, marketing services and speaking engagements. He is a quintessential connector and problem-solving savant.

Jeff's entrepreneurial pursuits have been recognized as Business of the Year by Brevard County, INC. 500 Fastest Growth Companies, Grow FL "Top 50 Companies to Watch" and the Boy Scouts Golden Eagle Award. As a former award-winning college basketball coach, he was presented the Atlanta Tip-Off Club Coach of the Year.

Jeff and his wife of 35 years, Judy, live in Viera, Florida and have three children.

ERIC WRIGHT BIO

Eric Wright is an innovative leader, dynamic speaker and published author. He turns complex principles into simple and practical life applications. For over 25 years, Eric has taught leadership and management seminars on four continents, served on various economic development and visioning councils, and authored  hundreds of published articles and three books.

As President of Publishing at SCB Marketing, Eric oversees the production of four business and lifestyle journals, along with numerous specialty publications. Through these journals, Eric offers entrepreneurs and business leaders a trusted voice connecting communities across Florida and the U.S.

Eric and his wife, Susan, live in Indialantic, Florida, and have three married sons and four grandchildren.

CONNECT WITH THE AUTHORS

Do you need a keynote speaker or emcee for a seminar, company convention, commencement ceremony, or another event? Jeff Piersall and Eric Wright are inspirational leaders, innovative trailblazers and energetic speakers who motivate, encourage and support entrepreneurs and business leaders by educating them on the principles of *Dogs Don't Bark at Parked Cars* and how to drive scalable growth in a collaborative entrepreneurial ecosystem.

For interviews and speaking engagements contact:
Wendy Kurtz, APR, CPRC
President – Elizabeth Charles & Associates, LLC
P.O. Box 547252
Orlando, FL 32854-7252
407.876.7730
wkurtz@ElizabethCharles.com
www.WendyKurtz.com

To directly contact Jeff Piersall and Eric Wright:
SCB Marketing
321.622.5986
jeff@scbmarketing.com
eric@scbmarketing.com

For more information about *Dogs Don't Bark at Parked Cars*, please visit:
https://dogsdontbark.com/

And, don't forget to subscribe to the *Dogs Don't Bark at Parked Cars* newsletter!

Morgan James
Speakers Group

We connect Morgan James published
authors with live and online events
and audiences who will benefit
from their expertise.

 Morgan James makes all of our titles available
through the Library for All Charity Organization.

www.LibraryForAll.org

Printed in the USA
CPSIA information can be obtained
at www.ICGtesting.com
JSHW081452301023
51114JS00007B/360

9 781683 504467